IBN KHALDUN
ابن خلدون

Anthropology's Ancestors

Edited by **Aleksandar Bošković**, University of Belgrade; Institute of Archaeology, Belgrade; Max Planck Institute for Social Anthropology, Halle/Saale

As anthropology developed across geographical, historical, and social boundaries, it was always influenced by works of exceptional scholars who pushed research topics in new and original directions and who can be regarded as important ancestors of the discipline. The aim of this series is to offer introductions to these major figures, whose works constitute landmarks and are essential reading for students of anthropology but who are also of interest for scholars in the humanities and social sciences more generally. In doing so, it offers important insights into some of the basic questions facing humanity.

Volume 8
Ibn Khaldun
Lawrence Rosen

Volume 7
Elsdon Best
Jeffrey Paparoa Holman and Frederico Delgado Rosa

Volume 6
Max Gluckman
Hugh Macmillan

Volume 5
Alfred Cort Haddon: A Very English Savage
Ciarán Walsh

Volume 4
Mary Douglas
Paul Richards and Perri 6

Volume 3
Françoise Héritier
Gérald Gaillard

Volume 2
William Robertson Smith
Aleksandar Bošković

Volume 1
Margaret Mead
Paul Shankman

IBN
KHALDUN
ابن خلدون

• • •

Lawrence Rosen

berghahn
NEW YORK • OXFORD
www.berghahnbooks.com

First published in 2026 by
Berghahn Books
www.berghahnbooks.com

© 2026 Lawrence Rosen

All rights reserved. Except for the quotation of short passages
for the purposes of criticism and review, no part of this book
may be reproduced in any form or by any means, electronic or
mechanical, including photocopying, recording, or any information
storage and retrieval system now known or to be invented,
without written permission of the publisher.

Library of Congress Cataloging-in-Publication Data

A C.I.P. cataloging record is available from the Library of Congress
Library of Congress Cataloging in Publication Control Number: 2025032183

British Library Cataloguing in Publication Data

A catalogue record for this book is available from the British Library

EU GPSR Authorized Representative

LOGOS EUROPE, 9 rue Nicolas Poussin, 17000, LA ROCHELLE, France
Email: Contact@logoseurope.eu

ISBN 978-1-83695-195-7 hardback
ISBN 978-1-83695-194-0 paperback
ISBN 978-1-83695-193-3 epub
ISBN 978-1-83695-196-4 web pdf

https://doi.org/10.3167/9781836951957

For Terry Burke
Friend of my youth, friend for all time

Perhaps some later scholar, aided by the divine gifts of a sound mind and of solid scholarship, will penetrate into these problems in greater detail than we did here. He may gradually add more problems until the discipline I created is completely presented. Allah knows, and you do not know.

—Ibn Khaldun, *Muqaddima*

CONTENTS

List of Figures	x
Acknowledgments	xii
A Note on Transcription	xiii
Introduction. Ibn Khaldun and the Anthropological Enterprise	1
Chapter 1. Theory as Context: The Man and His Times	13
Chapter 2. Social Solidarity and the Theory of Cyclical History	36
Chapter 3. Free Will and the Individual in History	61
Chapter 4. The Anthropology of Religion: Inner States and Overt Acts	83
Chapter 5. Shari'a, Custom, and the Anthropology of Law	99
Chapter 6. Ibn Khaldun as an Arab Thinker	122
Conclusion. The Allure of the Universal, the Tug of the Particular	133
Selected Works by Ibn Khaldun	137
References	139
Index	155

FIGURES

0.1. Representations of Ibn Khaldun. Wikimedia Commons; Shutterstock; Pinterest, public domain.   7

1.1. For centuries, Christians and Muslims fought for control of North Africa and the Iberian Peninsula. Wikimedia Commons, public domain.   15

1.2. Ibn Khaldun traveled widely, from Spain and North Africa to Egypt and the holy sites of the Middle East. By permission of "Fundación El Legado Andalusí."   17

1.3. Ibn Khaldun's friend Lisan al-Khatib was murdered by his political opponents. Available at https://alchetron.com/Ibn-al-Khatib. Public domain.   20

1.4. On the basis of fragmentary remains, Russian anthropologist Mikhail Garasimov recreated the appearance of Tamerlane. Photograph: Alexander Liskin, Sputnik. Available at https://sputnikmediabank.com/media/787185.html?context=list&list_sid=list_1003654.   25

1.5. Rembrandt based a drawing of the meeting of Ibn Khaldun and Tamerlane on an Indian portrayal.   26

1.6. Tamerlane destroyed the city of Damascus notwithstanding the efforts of Ibn Khaldun to reach a peaceful takeover. Available at https://ballandalus.wordpress.com/2014/08/30/the-scholar-and-the-sultan-a-translation-of-the-historic-encounter-between-ibn-khaldun-and-timur/. Public domain.   27

4.1. Manuals for the practice of magic were common in Ibn Khaldun's world, though he argued against their use in policy decisions. Wikimedia Commons, public domain. 87

4.2. Jews and Muslims playing chess was an illustration of the relation between the two confessional communities in Spain and North Africa. Wikimedia Commons, public domain. 90

4.3. Notwithstanding his attachments to Sufism, it is unclear whether Ibn Khaldun frequented their prayer rituals. Wikimedia Commons, public domain. 92

5.1. Ibn Khaldun refused to dress like the judges of Mamluk Egypt. Available at https://bibliotecanatalie.com/f/de-medici-da-vinci-and-mamluk-sultan-qaitbay?blogcategory=Arab. Public domain. 101

5.2. In this document Ibn Khaldun's signature can be seen in the upper left-hand corner. Wikimedia Commons, public domain. 102

5.3. The Circle of Justice represents the elements that make possible a peaceful and successful community of believers. Available at https://ballandalus.wordpress.com/2016/07/21/ibn-hajar-al-asqalanis-biography-of-ibn-khaldun-d-8081406/. Public domain. 116

ACKNOWLEDGMENTS

Discussions with numerous colleagues have played a key role in my approach to Ibn Khaldun. Akbar Ahmed, who holds a chair in his name, has not only reinforced our understanding of Ibn Khaldun's relevance to present-day Muslims but has, in his own courageous endeavors, demonstrated that, like his predecessor, one can be an insightful scholar and a thoughtful diplomat simultaneously. Abdellah Hammoudi has shown me the continuing influence of Ibn Khaldun's thinking about tribal history and has, in so many ways over the years, never failed to share his astute comprehension of all things anthropological. Over the course of many years, I was the recipient of the generosity of Clifford and Hildred Geertz, Ernest Gellner, and David Hart, and the memories of our conversations, while not always apparent, resonate throughout this book. I am also grateful to Aleksandar Bošković, who invited my contribution to this series, and Lahouari Touati, who prompted me to think about Ibn Khaldun's ideas on free will, for their ongoing encouragement. I feel the shared ideas of each of these scholars and friends not as the burden of an ongoing debt but as an enduring and uplifting gift. Finally, a special note of thanks to Barbara Cooper for her help in choosing the illustrations for this book, Kathryn Dillon at the Witherle Memorial Library for her expert assistance with the illustrations and research materials, and all the townsfolk of Castine, Maine, for their warm welcome.

The book is dedicated to Edmund (Terry) Burke, III. As fellow graduate students, we worked together in the Middle Atlas Mountains of Morocco on tribal history, and in all the following years Terry has been an unrivaled source of wisdom about our shared interests. His own work on tribal and world history would,

I have no doubt, been of enormous interest to Ibn Khaldun. For his knowledge and his friendship, I am eternally grateful.

Finally, it is customary for authors to take full responsibility for any errors contained in their books, however much we would prefer to settle any remaining blame on our interlocutors. I will take as my version of this absolution the words with which Ibn Khaldun (1969: 9) concludes his foreword to the *Muqaddima*, in the hope that, by association, I may benefit from my own readers' forgiveness and understanding:

> I wish that men of scholarly competence and wide knowledge would look at the book with a critical, rather than a complacent eye, and silently correct or overlook the mistakes they come upon. The capital of knowledge that an individual scholar has to offer is small. Admission (of one's shortcomings) saves from censure. Kindness from colleagues is hoped for. It is God whom I ask to make our deeds acceptable in His sight. He is a good protector.

* * *

A Note on Transcription

Arabic words are transliterated following the style employed in Hans Wehr's *A Dictionary of Modern Written Arabic*, with some modification for terms used in colloquial Moroccan Arabic (*darija*). Generally, the first time an Arabic word appears, full diacritics will be used; thereafter they may not. Readers should also be aware that transliterated spellings vary in the literature: For example, *'asabiya* is often rendered *'asabiyya*, and *Muqaddima* as *Muqaddimah*. Some Arabic terms that are commonly used in English (e.g., Quran, shari'a) as well as familiar Arabic names may be transliterated in an Anglicized form that readers will have no difficulty recognizing. Dates are given in the Western form.

INTRODUCTION
IBN KHALDUN AND THE ANTHROPOLOGICAL ENTERPRISE

● ● ●

Perhaps an epoch is not quite long enough,
nor a single lifetime,
for pattern and order to emerge from numbers.
Better to look from far away.
—Tomasz Różycki, *To The Letter*

Ibn Khaldun (1332–1406 CE) is not the father of anthropology. While some sociologists claim him for their own, even those anthropologists who are familiar with his writings are more likely to regard him as a distant relative than a direct progenitor. Why, then, include him as an ancestor of the discipline?

To answer that inquiry, one first has to ask: What is distinctive about anthropology? What are its key assumptions, its ways of framing questions, its intellectual hopes and proffered goals? To those concerns, a recognizable response is readily forthcoming. For if anthropology stands for anything among the disciplines, it stands for three things in particular: the willingness to seek through highly detailed study the patterns that inform the daily life of ordinary people, to connect diverse domains of social and cultural life that other disciplines may unwisely segregate, and to place oneself at once within the society as an unassuming participant and stand back long enough to be a dispassionate observer.

It is the argument of this study that Ibn Khaldun not only broke with the ways in which history was previously portrayed—both in the Muslim world and in the West—but that he set in play the elements from which a rigorous anthropology was imaginable, and with it a process whose contributions continue to resonate well beyond the most readily available of his theories.

Given such an emphasis, the strategy of the present assessment may appear to take a somewhat roundabout course. Most accounts of his work focus almost exclusively on Ibn Khaldun's well-known cyclical theory of history—solidary tribes, forged in the cauldron of religious ardor and kin-based ideology, come roaring out of the margins to capture the center only to become the victims of its decadent ways and unavoidable decline. But Ibn Khaldun's approach, however much it appears to incorporate ineluctable forces, is fraught with subtle ambiguities, features that lead him to see connections among cultural domains his forerunners ignored, features that render his overall account far from simply deterministic. Seeking connections is indispensable to his whole approach: "It is obvious," he writes, "that it is from the relations existing among the data that one finds out the unknown from the known" (Ibn Khaldun 1969: 89). Indeed, his style of making those linkages, though not unrelated to his uses of classical Western thought, has to be understood in its own terms if his ideas are not to be either trivialized or domesticated.

Moreover, since much about his life is unknown, and he did not always supply answers to the questions he raised, our analysis must needs be somewhat speculative. Perhaps an appropriately cautious account would not stray into such territory. However, there are several reasons why at moments I shall. First, because in doing so one may see connections previously unnoticed, connections that may help fill in the blanks of the materials we possess. Second, Ibn Khaldun himself commends the use of speculation (*naẓar*) as a vehicle for gaining insight, so perhaps a certain degree of informed guesswork might even have met with his approval. Finally, trying to read between the lines not only may stimulate new insights into Ibn Khaldun's available thought but may demonstrate how his mode of thinking does indeed serve as an ancestral source for ways in which we might carry on his project.

We will, then, organize this analysis along three main lines: First, while dividing Ibn Khaldun's contribution into familiar domains—his theory of history, his approaches to tribal organization, mysticism, law, and politics—we will, in fact, be looking constantly at his form of reasoning and how it relates features in a way consistent with his own culture's assumptions. Then, second, we will consider how his approach fits with—and stands distinct from—the predominant modes of analysis of his own day. Here, Ibn Khaldun's ideas about free will, causation, credible information, and oral versus written transmission will all be relevant to an understanding of his methodology and intent. Finally, we will consider how his mode of analysis has relevance for the ongoing anthropological enterprise. For just as his famous theory of history concentrates on recurrent themes, so, too, the theories to which anthropologists attach themselves have a way of receding and returning, thus often redirecting our attention in new and challenging ways to the sources of our current concerns.

As in any such undertaking—and particularly one that reaches back to an individual who lived over six hundred years ago—the sources and reliability of our information become crucial. Fortunately, most of Ibn Khaldun's major writings have been handed down intact over the centuries. The most important is the *Muqaddima*, written during his withdrawal from the world to the fortified site of Qala ben Salama, near the present-day village of Tiaret in northwestern Algeria. He says of that work: "[t]his book has become unique, as it contains unusual knowledge and familiar if hidden wisdom" (Ibn Khaldun 1969: 9). Although we will refer to some of his other writings, particularly those on Sufism and his *Autobiography*, it is to this work that our attention must necessarily be most closely directed.

The *Muqaddima*, written during a brief period of five months in 1377, is commonly referred to as the "Introduction" or "Prolegomena" to the multivolume work collectively entitled the *Kitab al-'Ibar* (Book of Lessons).[1] The "Introduction" contains the heart of Ibn Khaldun's cyclical theory of empires, while the following volumes deal mainly with the history of the Berber tribes of North Africa. A separate work is usually referred to as his *Autobiography*.[2] This latter may seem unusual, but autobiographies were not as uncommon in the medieval Arab world as some have assumed. Westerners may imagine that St. Augustine's *Confessions*, written at the end of the fourth century, initiated a form that was quickly adopted, but the truth is that more than a millennium passed before such self-reflective works reappeared in Europe. Meanwhile, in the Arab world, autobiographies were fairly widespread.[3] Biographies, too, were quite prevalent, their form being more settled than that of the autobiographies. But whether it was biography or autobiography, such works focused primarily on genealogical attachments and events as proof that the subject was indeed worthy of God's beneficence. What these accounts usually lacked was information about the individual's inner state, personal life, or generalizations about human nature and social forces drawn from personal experience. While chronology was not ignored, it was not taken as revelatory of individual dispositions or broad historical trajectories. And while, as we will see, Ibn Khaldun does not delve deeply into those features of personal identity that we think reveal a person's true self, he does, both by prescription and by example, demonstrate that his own rigorous analysis will not rest on those unverifiable features that characterized his predecessors' accounts.

How Ibn Khaldun, coming from a culture that placed heavy emphasis on individuality, related that factor to the forces of a universal history will also be of special interest. Although configured differently than in the West, the concept of the person and their relation to the unwinding of history is a vital aspect of understanding Ibn Khaldun's project. Why, we will ask, in such an intensely personalistic culture has he broken out to write about universal forces of history and not simply the deeds of individual men? Why, when biographical dictionaries in the Arab world were about family genealogy, military victories, and proofs of God's blessings, is he writing a "history of events"? Plutarch had described his own approach by saying, "It is not histories we are writing, but Lives" (Plutarch 1919: 7).[4] Notwithstanding his emphasis on impersonal forces, Ibn Khaldun, though in ways quite different from Plutarch and the ancients, still had to consider how character informs individual action—even (as he rather surprisingly notes) when it concerns proof of the Messiah's legitimacy. What is at work, as we will see, is not mindless fate, even though history, in his view, cannot escape elements of the inevitable. It is not even the spiritual suffusing the mundane—though the role of Sufi mysticism is vital to an understanding of his work—for one must still arise each morning and make decisions of uncertain consequence. Perhaps, in the end, for Ibn Khaldun the contradictions *are* the consequence—of free will and fortune, of force and cohesion, of person and surround—each outcome no less poignant for that reason. His contradictions may not be ours, but that he copes with them renders him a part of our present, and with it a challenge to how we, in turn, understand others' lives. By emphasizing deep structures, Ibn Khaldun set a course for the social sciences that anthropologists of various persuasions inherited even if they did not always acknowledge, or even know, they owed him a portion of that debt.

Moreover, it is not only the substance of what Ibn Khaldun has to say that is innovative but the way he matches his style to his form of explanation. While his mode of causal explanation will run as a theme throughout the present account, it is worth noting at the outset the connection between substance and presentation in his work. If, for example, you hold to a view of history focused on important leaders—or, as Margaret Mead once said, you believe that a small group of thoughtful, committed people can change the world—your account will look very different from one in which you think that destiny lies in biology, economics, or the environment. Where earlier Muslim historiography centered on a particular version of persons and events, Ibn Khaldun was critical of those representations and clearly set forth a very different set of criteria. How he approached the philosophy of the ancient Greeks and that of his more recent Muslim forebearers on questions of causality, personhood, and the natural world is vital to an understanding of what he sought to explain, to his novel form of historical narrative, and to the influence he has had on the development of the social sciences.

Ibn Khaldun's style of presentation is also no less important than his substantive claims. In his own day there were those who, though disagreeing with the substance of his analysis, saw great merit in its form of expression. Although his work was published and distributed in his lifetime—and was, along with his reputation as a diplomat and jurist, responsible for his being recognized in advance of his travels to various countries—Ibn Khaldun's theories have become more widely known outside of his own time and place than within them. Some people—both in the East and the West—have adopted Ibn Khaldun's cyclical view of history either as a way of claiming their own exception to it or as a way of gauging where they and others may be on the cycle, whether for purposes of taxation, expansion, or foreign relations. The Ottomans, for example, cited him in order to claim they were the exception to inevitable decline and some colonial regimes used his theory to justify their domination of societies they believed only the West could save from the decay he predicted, while Naguib Mahfouz (in his novel *Harafish*) could take the opposite tack and suggest that colonial regimes would be the ones to follow Ibn Khaldun's dynasts into inevitable decline.

In the West, Ibn Khaldun's work was not very widely known until the mid-twentieth century when a number of translations and critiques of his writings became available.[5] A huge boost to his recognition came in 1948 with the discussion of his work by Arnold Toynbee who, in his best-seller *A Study of History*, characterized Ibn Khaldun as "an Arabic genius" comparable to Thucydides and Machiavelli, someone who, in the *Muqaddima*, produced "undoubtedly the greatest work of its kind that has ever yet been created by any mind in any time or place."[6] Translations into various European languages have also brought Ibn Khaldun's writings to a larger audience, while critical studies by Muhsin Mahdi, Abdeslam Chaddadi, Allen James Fromherz, Aziz al-Azmeh, and Robert Irwin have only increased his visibility.[7]

On the more popular level, one can point to Mark Zuckerberg's choice of the *Muqaddima* as a must-read and Ronald Reagan's glowing reference to his theory of taxation, while among science fiction writers, one can cite the influence of Ibn Khaldun on Frank Herbert's *Dune* and Isaac Asimov's *Foundation*. Even Nobel Laureate Paul Krugman (2013), after saying of the *Muqaddima* that "it truly is an awesome work, centuries ahead of its time," referred to Asimov's economist character Hari Seldon as showing that "Ibn Khaldun was setting himself up to be the Hari Seldon of medieval Islam. And he did a pretty good job!"[8] Arab

Figure 0.1. Representations of Ibn Khaldun. Wikimedia Commons; Shutterstock; Pinterest, public domain.

nationalists have also been drawn to Ibn Khaldun as an exemplar of indigenous scholarship and political astuteness. Thus, on the six hundredth anniversary of his death, numerous exhibitions and celebrations took place in Europe and various Muslim countries. Statues, stamps, commemorative plates, endowed professorships, a television comedy, and entire universities honoring him can now be found in many parts of the world.

Among anthropologists, Ibn Khaldun's work had an impact on various scholars, most notably Ernest Gellner and Akbar Ahmed, but also Philip Salzman, Talal Asad, and Mahmood Mamdani; among sociologists, Emile Durkheim, Pitrim Sorokin, and Robert E. Park regarded him as vital to the development of their discipline, while Eric Hobsbawm called him "the greatest social and historical mind of the medieval world." Grand scale history employing anthropology has, in the work of such writers as Yuval Harari, Edward O. Wilson, Jared Diamond, Harvey Whitehouse, and others, focused largely on biology, ecology, and economics, cyclical theories being less popular than traditional straight-line accounts. Nevertheless, Ibn Khaldun's work underscores two issues that anthropologists and others have always had to face.

The first relates to the tension between those classical rivals, the universal and the particular. As ethnographers, anthropologists confront the minutiae of everyday life in a wide range of societies yet remain tempted by grand theories—structuralism, cultural evolution, functionalism, etc.—that speak to more encompassing aspects of the human condition. As we will see, it is a tension Ibn Khaldun knew well. The second problem concerns alternative rationalities. Here the issue is whether perception, reasoning, and worldview differ fundamentally across cultures or respond to the same underlying traits and historical forces. A. M. Hocart put this dilemma quite succinctly when he said: "How can we make any progress in the understanding of cultures, ancient or modern, if we persist in dividing what people join, and in joining what they keep apart?"[9] Ibn Khaldun understood that cultural differences were not simply erased by the commonalities of imperial history, but it is an open question how exactly he related individual accomplishment and impersonal events. Whether in his quest to reconcile his mystical beliefs with his unvarnished account of the politics of empires or his recognition that his own North African heritage did not map exactly onto the culture of Mamluk Egypt, Ibn Khaldun recognized—and in his own life exemplified—an approach to the very problems succeeding generations of anthropologists would also have to face. Each of the following chapters will, therefore, be aimed at drawing us ever more closely to the topics and methods through which Ibn Khaldun seeks the universal while attending carefully to the particular.

Immanuel Kant once said that "experience without theory is blind, but theory without experience is mere intellectual play." In chapter 1 we will review the extraordinary life of Ibn Khaldun in an effort to recapture the context in which he came to construct his theory of history—from his travails as a political adviser to his personal losses during the years of the Black Death, his encounter with Tamerlane, and his return to the fraught world of Mamluk Egypt. For this incomparably practical man, a universe of insurmountable forces had to be reconciled with a mystical faith, and the two had to confront a world at once preordained and subject to human effect.

Ibn Khaldun is hardly the only one who has seen cyclical movement in the unfolding of time: We all observe the rotating seasons; we all see birth and maturation and decline. But whereas many cultures—particularly those of the Christian West—see time as directional and history as if not purposive at least not subject to reflux, Ibn Khaldun saw patterns beneath events and with them a vision of how humankind was embedded in forces at once governing and manipulable. In chapter 2 we will, therefore, see how environment, economic forces, and social solidarity inform Ibn Khaldun's view of the history of empires and humanity's placement among them.

Muslims are not fatalists. Since "knowledge" is the second most frequently used word in the Quran (after the name of God) and must be sought "even unto China," it is incumbent on all Believers to exercise their God-given powers of reason to overcome their passions and achieve a viable community of the faithful. Yet context matters and no one is entirely free from external constraints. Like others before him, Ibn Khaldun had to ask: Do we possess free will or is it, as Isaac Bashevis Singer once quipped, that "we have to believe in free will, we have no choice"? Chapter 3 will seek to understand this conundrum from Ibn Khaldun's perspective as both a Sufi adherent and a worldly jurist and political operative.

Neither in the *Muqaddima* nor even in the *Autobiography* does Ibn Khaldun concentrate on his inner feelings and thoughts. Yet that inward turn is vital to his religious orientation as a Sufi and with it to an understanding of how he would have us imagine an individual's position in his times. For him, as we will see in chapter 4, that mystic world is not a denial or retreat from the messiness of everyday personal and political life but an indissoluble link to it, as necessary to completion of a fractured existence as it is to the desired course of human affairs.

On multiple occasions Ibn Khaldun served as a judge. Although records of his decisions have not survived, his views on the law can be teased out of his writings and the broader socio-religious environment within which he operated. Of particular interest in chapter 5 will be his approach to customary practices, an emphasis that often takes precedence over the strictures of formal Islamic law. Thus, in the course of placing his views of the law in the broader context of his studies, we will see Ibn Khaldun's mode of bringing his theories of causation, facts, and events into a realm where uncertainty reigns but decisions must nevertheless be forthcoming.

It is imperative to keep in mind that Ibn Khaldun is deeply embedded in Arab culture. His assumptions, his categories, his modes of assessing others and their situations, however influenced by outside concepts, are invariably enmeshed in those of his Arab cultural heritage. In chapter 6 we will, therefore, return to several assumptions about persons and actions found in his work with the focus clearly on their distinctively Arab framing and employment—and his own creative departures from them.

Aimé Césaire has spoken of "a universal rich with all that is particular." Accordingly, the final portion of the book will bring us back to the central question of how Ibn Khaldun copes with the allure of the universal and the tug of the particular. In doing so we can relate features of his work that may seem inconsistent and underscore why his approach to this issue remains, across more than six centuries, a beacon for anthropologists who have followed in his wake.

NOTES

1. The full title is *Kitāb al-'Ibar wa-Dīwān al-Mubtada' wa-l-Khabar fī Ta'rīkh al-'Arab wa-l-Barbar wa-Man 'Āṣarahum min Dhawī ash-Sha'n al-Akbār* (Book of lessons, record of beginnings and events in the history of the Arabs and the Berbers and their powerful contemporaries). The Arabic word *muqaddima* has also been translated as "premise" (Gule 2015: 8) and "allusions" (El-Rayes 2013).
2. The full title is *at-Ta'rīf bi-ibn Khaldūn wa-Riḥlatih Gharban wa-Sharqan* (Presenting Ibn Khaldun and his journey west and east). There is no complete translation of the *Autobiography* into English. For excerpts see, Alatas 2013, Ballan 2014, and Fischel 1952.
3. See Reynolds 2001, Ghamdi 1989, and Kilpatrick 1991. On biographies, see Hourani 1991: 165–66.
4. In his famous statement near the beginning of "The Life of Alexander," Plutarch (1919: 7) says: "I am writing biography, not history, and the truth is that the most brilliant exploits often tell us nothing of the virtues or vices of the men who performed them, while on the other hand a chance remark or a joke may reveal far more of a man's character than the mere feat of winning battles in which thousands fall, or of marshalling great armies, or laying siege to cities."
5. Unless otherwise indicated, for purposes of this study the translation of the *Muqaddima* by Franz Rosenthal (Ibn Khaldun 1969) will be used, even though that version has been subject to some criticism. Few anthropologists will need to go beyond the abridged version of Rosenthal's translation.
6. See Toynbee 1934: 321–28 and 1954: 84–87. Toynbee's work was so popular that he was even featured on the cover of the 17 March 1947 issue of *Time* magazine. In response to the attention the story garnered, the publisher later wrote:

    The governors of seven states have been heard from, as have businessmen, Congressmen, plain citizens, radio broadcasters, journalists (Wrote Edgar Ansel Mowrer. *New York Post* columnist and foreign affairs expert: "Never before, in my judgment, has any American magazine printed anything quite as important . . ."). In particular, the clergy has been strongly represented—the General Commission on Army and Navy Chaplains, for example, having requested 1,700 reprints for distribution to Armed Forces chaplains everywhere.

For critiques of Toynbee's approach to Ibn Khaldun, see Irwin 1997; see generally, Montague 1956.

7. Similarly, Hugh Trevor-Roper praised Ibn Khaldun's analysis as "subtle deep and formless as the ocean" (cited in Ruthven 2019). However, the claim by Bruce Lawrence (1983: 157) that his rediscovery by Western scholars demonstrates that "Ibn Khaldun is a product of Orientalism and the extent to which he can be assessed apart from the Orientalist interest evoked by him is highly questionable" overstates the case, particularly since that rediscovery was also carried out by a number of Muslim scholars. On the variety of Western readers' interpretations of Ibn Khaldun's writings see, Abdesselem 1983.

8. On the Reagan quote, see chapter 2. For Krugman's reference to Ibn Khaldun, see Krugman 2013. Zuckerberg (2015) wrote:

    My next book for *A Year of Books* is *Muqaddam* by Ibn Khaldun. It's a history of the world written by an intellectual who lived in the 1300s. It focuses on how society and culture flow, including the creation of cities, politics, commerce and science.

    While much of what was believed then is now disproven after 700 more years of progress, it's still very interesting to see what was understood at this time and the overall worldview when it's all considered together.

9. Hocart (1952) 1970: 23.

CHAPTER 1
THEORY AS CONTEXT
THE MAN AND HIS TIMES

● ● ●

There is no theory that is not a fragment,
carefully prepared, of some autobiography.
—Paul Valéry

If the times are just one day is for me
and one day is against me.
—Medjoub "The Sarcastic"

Which opening scene for the film version of Ibn Khaldun's life would you choose? Would it be the sight of bodies, including those of the subject's own parents, struck down by the Black Death in fourteenth-century Tunisia? Or the storm at sea that took the lives of his wife and daughters? Would it be of our hero first bribing and then leading into battle nomadic tribesmen—forced in one campaign even to eat his own horse? Or should the film open on one of the prison cells in which he awaited a change of regimes? Would it be more fitting to start with a view of the writer in his aerie above the cave-dwellers of western Algeria during the four years he retreated from the world to prepare his great study of human history? Or should the movie flash back to that night when he was lowered down the city walls to enter the camp of Tamerlane, the greatest "barbarian" warrior of his day, to parlay over peace and the science of history? And who would you want playing him: Sean Connery? Alec Guinness? Omar Sharif?

Or could no one person or incident capture the life and thought of one of Western scholarship's favorite figures of the medieval Muslim world, the ever-elusive Ibn Khaldun?

To the scholarly community, Ibn Khaldun is at once familiar and distant. Best known for his theory of the cyclical rise and fall of Arab and Berber dynasties, Ibn Khaldun has at times caught the notice of popularizers only to recede into relative obscurity as his views are occulted by the shifting taste in historical and anthropological explanation. It is not, however, necessary to choose between seeing him only as a generalist or a particularist, a figure of his age or a "modern" thinker who just happened to live six hundred years ago. Rather, in introducing him to social scientists who are not conversant with his thinking, a bit of each feature would not be out of order. His story is one of a man in his moment and of a man who broke with the scholars of his day to see matters in ways that are familiar in our own era. It is a story that entwines personal experience with the ways in which he sought a theory that would make sense of the world around him.[1]

His full name was Abū Zayd 'Abd ar-Raḥmān ibn Muḥammad ibn Khaldūn al-Ḥaḍramī. Born on 27 May 1332 (at the start of the Muslim fasting month of Ramadan), he carried, along with his other identifiers, the name Hadrami as an indication of his family's roots in the Hadhramaut region of the Arabian Peninsula. And yet Ibn Khaldun seems to have been of several minds about his own descent. For he not only criticized others for their pretensions to a noble pedigree but was at times both proud and skeptical of his personal genealogy as well as often being more favorably disposed to the Berbers of North Africa than his Arab progenitors.[2] What is clear is that his ancestors emigrated from the heartland of Islam to Andalusian Spain in the eighth century where many of them served in—and were subject to the machinations of—successive dynasties. Around the time of the partial reconquest by Christian forces in 1248 the family moved to Tunisia.[3]

Whether in North Africa or in Spain, whether in the early days of the Arab invasion or at the time of his birth, the world of Ibn Khaldun's family was more often than not both turbulent and

Figure 1.1. For centuries, Christians and Muslims fought for control of North Africa and the Iberian Peninsula. Wikimedia Commons, public domain.

alluring. Already as a young man Ibn Khaldun experienced two factors that became central to his later theorizing—the similar trajectories of the dynasties under which he lived and the fortuitous events that shaped their course.

Tunisia, along with most of North Africa and the Iberian Peninsula, had by the mid-fourteenth century been witness to the rise and fall of several Berber dynasties. Each arose from the margins of a predecessor civilization, each employed tribal heritage and its own brand of Islam to consolidate support and pursue an expansionist agenda. To follow, at least in summary form, the life of Ibn Khaldun in terms of the fluctuations of his era is to gain some insight into the matters he ultimately felt the need to comprehend. What follows, then, is but a brief synopsis of Ibn Khaldun's biography, the thrust of which is to sense how much the context of his troubled times set the course for the issues he sought to understand as an historian.

Three main Berber dynasties marked the medieval period in North Africa. The Almoravid dynasty, which held sway from 1050 until 1147, arose out of the western Sahara and, moving ever northward, exhibited many of the features common to each of its successors: rapid expansion into settled territories and major urban centers, internal struggles often resulting in internecine bloodshed, the construction of monumental (mainly religious) edifices, the creation of courtly retinues whose scholars and artisans followed the latest patron, and ever-growing dependence on subalterns who came from outside the core of the founders. At the edge of the Almoravids lay the next rival, the Almohads, who, during a reign lasting from 1147 to 1215, claimed greater fidelity to the unity of God while rallying the tribes of the High Atlas Mountains to conquer much of northwest Africa and the southern provinces of the Iberian Peninsula. Notwithstanding stark differences with their predecessors, the Almohad shared many traits with the Almoravid, including intrafamilial murder and stunning architecture. By the time of Ibn Khaldun's birth, however, they too had been displaced by the Merinid dynasty (1244–1465).

For the young Ibn Khaldun such dynastic travails were, if not yet at the forefront of his concerns, not irrelevant to the education he received and the issues he would eventually have to face. Coming from a comfortable family with a long history of involvement in Islamic studies Ibn Khaldun received instruction from a number of the finest scholars who, like his own family, had fled Spain and settled in the major cities of North Africa. He learned to recite the Quran by heart and, under the tutelage of the rationalist scholar Muhammad al-Abili, was taught, in addition to Islamic jurisprudence, logic, and the Arab sciences, two things that remained with him for life: one should travel widely and see for oneself, and one should not rely on what can be found in books but engage in direct contact with teachers and personal study of original sources.[4]

In 1349, at the age of seventeen while deeply devoted to his studies, the first of many tragedies he was to endure struck in the form of the Black Death.

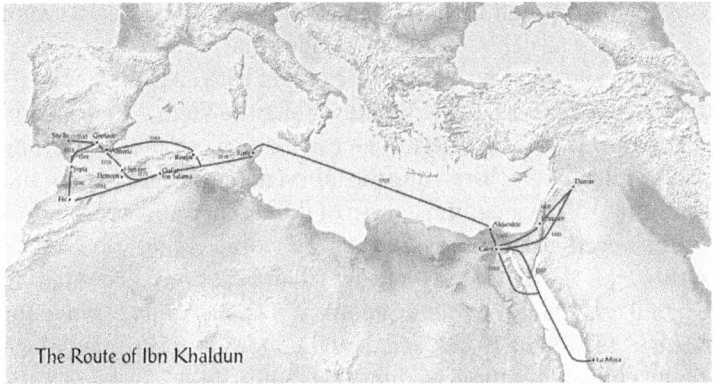

Figure 1.2. Ibn Khaldun traveled widely, from Spain and North Africa to Egypt and the holy sites of the Middle East. By permission of "Fundación El Legado Andalusí."

Bubonic plague arrived in North Africa, as it did throughout the Mediterranean and Europe with devastating effect. It killed 40 to 60 percent of the population of Europe, whereas the figures for North Africa may have been comparable in the cities but appear to have been much lower in the countryside (see Singer 2020). Later, Ibn Khaldun wrote:

> The pestilence that beset civilization east and west in the mid-fourteenth century decimated communities and wiped out the mountain people. Many of the beauties of civilized society were swallowed up and erased. As mankind diminished in size, so too did the earth's civilization. Garrisons and workshops were destroyed; pathways and landmarks vanished. Entire regions and houses were emptied; regimes and tribes were weakened. The entire population changed. The same fate befell both the eastern and the western regions, the difference being only matters of degree and the extent to which the region was urbanized. It was as if the entire discourse of existence had pronounced the words apathy and gloom, and the response had come in a rush.[5]

Tearing through Ibn Khaldun's world the Black Death swept aside almost all of his teachers and killed both of his parents, leading him to conclude: "It folded the carpet with all there was on it" (quoted in Enan 1979: 9). Whatever else the young Ibn Khaldun learned from the experience, he carried forever after the strong feeling that, notwithstanding the inherent tendencies of men and dynasties to run a natural course of florescence and decline, fortuitous events can utterly change the world. As he was later to write, "the things that are accidental and cannot be counted on . . . must inevitably produce an event peculiar to its essence [or nature] as well as to the accidental conditions that may attach themselves to it" (Ibn Khaldun 1969: 38, 1958: 1:72).

The Merinid dynasty was at its height at the time of Ibn Khaldun's birth. Arising from a faction of the tribal confederation of the Berber Zenata of western Algeria, the Merinids had been pushed by rivals into Morocco where they consolidated their administration before striking back across northwestern Africa and parts of Spain only to endure the fate of their predecessors as battles with Christians and various Arab groups began to whittle away at their dominance. Yet in the mid-fourteenth century, the Merinid Empire still afforded clear opportunities for the politically ambitious, and Ibn Khaldun, eager to become involved with whoever prevailed at the moment, was quick to seek out inclusion.

His first opportunity came when he was appointed as a scribe in the court in Tunis. However, when the Marinid ruler Abu 'Inan (who had deposed his father and whose own vizier later had him strangled) invaded the country Ibn Khaldun was quick to accept a post at his court in Fez. Although he regarded the position as beneath him, the job nevertheless brought him face-to-face with the risks involved in seeking one's advantage in a universe of intrigue and betrayal. For within two years of arriving in Morocco, Ibn Khaldun conspired against the ruling sultan who, after recovering from what some thought was his death bed, sent him to prison for the next two years. The sultan was, however, prepared to release him when Ibn Khaldun composed an obsequious poem that read in part: "How can I remonstrate with time / And which vicissitudes of fortune can I fight? / I am submitting to the judgment of fate / Which at one time is favorable and at another antagonistic."[6] When the sultan suddenly died before Ibn Khaldun could be released, the vizier taking charge freed him, at which point Ibn Khaldun returned the favor by first siding with the vizier and then with his rivals before landing in the graces of an altogether new sultan who appointed him chief judge ruling on non-religious cases. These early experiences augured a pattern of intrigue and a quest for the victorious that was to run as a theme throughout Ibn Khaldun's career and others' assessments of him.

Indeed, the comments by his contemporaries and later scholars often turn not simply on his ideas but on his character and behavior. To some he was seen as a brilliant teacher and an unusually honest judge, while others have seen him as unprincipled and devious.[7] M. A. Enan (1979: 21, 39), for example, regards his pattern of looking only to the victors as evidence of his "wicked feelings and passions," thus marking him as someone who "did not hesitate to return evil for good," a man of "exaggerated egoism . . . who exhibited deep despise of sentiment and moral principles," an "opportunist using all sorts of means and methods . . . and to [whom] the end justified the means." Although even in the *Autobiography* Ibn Khaldun rarely revealed his inner feelings he does say, in a striking passage that may have been literally true of himself or intended as deeply sardonic, that: "Happiness and profit are achieved mostly by people who are obsequious and use flattery. Such character disposition is one of the reasons for happiness" (Ibn Khaldun 1958: 328). Surely there were times, particularly during the later years in Egypt, when he was openly provocative in his words or demeanor, thus precipitating the hostility of his colleagues. And surely he always sought to be on the side of the winners. His own family's history had long since indicated the price to be paid for winding up on the wrong side. His great-grandfather was serving as the finance minister for the ruler of the Hafsid dynasty in Tunis when he was tortured and executed by a rival to the throne, while Ibn Khaldun's grandfather retired from his posts in order to avoid the possibility of a similar fate during a comparable period of turbulence. Thus, given the machinations of those among whom he moved and the limited range of contemporary sources and lack of self-analysis with which we must contend perhaps reserving judgment of the man may not be wholly inappropriate. Mohammed Talbi (1971: 826), referring to the days when a twenty-year old Ibn Khaldun was in his first post in Fez, strikes a similar note when he says that North Africa at that time "was then in the process of disintegration and whose court furthermore was far from providing an example of loyalty and good behavior." That is especially relevant as we seek, in the years that followed the Black Death, to trace the course of Ibn Khaldun's thinking through the traces of his movements.

Following the death of his latest patron, Ibn Khaldun, ever mindful of the uncertainties of remaining in Tunisia, left for his ancestral home of Andalusia. There, at the invitation of the reigning sultan, he was sent to parley with the Christian king of Castile Pedro the Cruel. It was the first major experience Ibn Khaldun undertook as a negotiator but it was certainly not to be his last.

Figure 1.3. Ibn Khaldun's friend Lisan al-Khatib was murdered by his political opponents. Available at https://alchetron.com/Ibn-al-Khatib. Public domain.

It is also recorded that he was married and had two children by this time but, as would be true on so many occasions, he sent them elsewhere (in this instance to Constantine, in present-day Algeria), perhaps realizing, as became the case in later years, that they might be used as a lever to force him to do a ruler's bidding.[8] It was also at this time in Spain that he became close to Lisan ad-Din Ibn al-Khatib. The two men had met earlier in Fez where they formed a friendship based on similar background and talents.

Al-Khatib spoke highly of his friend, calling Ibn Khaldun "a man of virtue," "a veritable paragon of the Maghrib region."[9] As a prolific author, al-Khatib wrote on such diverse topics as poetry and agriculture, music, and the plague as a contagious disease (Ballan 2019, 2023). Although his relationship with Ibn Khaldun was uneven, they both viewed history as an artifact of human action, both became involved in political cabals, and both held a rather bleak view of the world they inhabited.[10]

Although the sultan showed great favor to Ibn Khaldun, his association with the intrigues of al-Khatib led Ibn Khaldun, in 1364, to seek the ruler's permission to depart Spain and accept the invitation of the Emir of Bougie (present-day Béjaïa, Algeria) to serve as manager of a wide variety of state affairs, not least the handling of relations with the local tribes. The Emir was part of the Hafsid dynasty of the region, a dynasty to which Ibn Khaldun was distantly related and which, in the chaotic rivalry of the times, was at times a client of or rival to the Merinids and other contenders for power. So, it is not surprising that, more intrigue and violence being the order of the day, after his latest patron was killed, Ibn Khaldun fled to the Emir's brother-in-law who appointed him to a similar post recruiting the local tribes. As one insurrection followed another, Ibn Khaldun eventually found himself the captive of the Merinid sultan of Morocco who had invaded the region from his home base in Fez. Promising he would assist in conquering the territory of his former employer, Ibn Khaldun was forgiven by the sultan for his past loyalty to the sultan's Hafsid rivals and was directed by him to bring the Berber tribesmen within the fold. When, however, the sultan in turn died, Ibn Khaldun retreated with his family to Fez where, following yet more intrigues and another brief imprisonment, he was forced to leave his family behind and cross back to Andalusia.

But conspiracies continued to follow him. His sometime friend al-Khatib, having chosen the wrong side in an ensuing contestation, fled to Morocco where his enemies charged him with heresy and then had him tortured and murdered in his prison cell in 1374. The loss of al-Khatib—whose life Ibn Khaldun had tried to save and whose actions only bought him the enmity of the Andalusian sultan—must have counted as yet another instance of both personal loss and the dangers of holding an appointed office. Expelled to North Africa by the sultan of Grenada for his ties to his friend, Ibn Khaldun was again obliged, to his considerable chagrin, to assist the local ruler in recruiting to his side the recalcitrant tribes. Given his involvement in these incessant trials, Talbi (1971: 827) summarizes how Ibn Khaldun was viewed by many at this time:

> He had become a political personality with a reputation that could not fail to arouse mistrust. He was henceforward condemned to offer his services for hire, and to be regarded with mixed feelings never entirely free from suspicion, whereas his only ambition now was to be left in peace to work out the conclusions to be drawn from his tumultuous experience and to put his ideas in order.

Indeed, he said: "I was in fact cured of the temptation of office. Furthermore I had for too long neglected scholarly matters. I therefore ceased to involve myself in the affairs of kings and devoted all my energies to study and teaching" (quoted from the *Ta'rif* in Talbi 1971: 826–27). Eventually he was able to prevail on one of the local officials to help him sever his ties with the sultan and assist him in finding a haven where he could retire at the age of forty-five from the world. And so, for the next four years (1375–79) he settled in the castle at Ibn Salama where he composed the *Muqaddima*, his great work on the history of the dynasties of North Africa.

Of the years he spent writing the *Muqaddima* we know rather little. He appears to have been very welcome among the Arab tribesmen of the region, but he tells us almost nothing about his daily life or inner thoughts. As Stephen Frederic Dale (2015: 140–41) notes:

> What is remarkable, astonishing even, about his memoire for this period is that he devotes less than one hundred words to this entire period and only a single sentence to the *Muqaddimah*. The sentence, though, at least suggests something of his intellectual excitement for what he recalled as a supremely creative "moment" in the late summer and autumn of 1377. In those few months, he reports, words and ideas came pouring from his mind, flowing like cream from a pitcher into a churn, to produce an *al-nahw al-gharib*, an "extraordinary method," the first draft of his philosophical history and science of man.

In this relatively isolated redoubt, Ibn Khaldun had to rely on the materials he had personally collected or could recall from his studies and personal experience. Meanwhile, his brother replaced him in some of his prior activities. A historian and poet in his own right, Ibn Khaldun's brother Abu Yahya had, in the years Ibn Khaldun was pressured to work for the Hafsid ruler, been sent by Ibn Khaldun to serve in his place. But involvement in politics was no less dangerous for Yahya than for his brother. Intrigue led to imprisonment, the confiscation of his property, and ultimately to his murder in 1378. Whatever his deepest feelings about the loss of his brother, ensconced in his citadel, Ibn Khaldun completed the *Prolegomena* in a short time and proceeded with his multivolume dynastic history. He says that he concentrated on the dynasties of Barbary "owing to my limited knowledge of the conditions of the East and its nations," although in subsequent revisions he added references to a number of other regimes. In a later ode he described the *Muqaddima* in the following terms:

> Here in the histories of time and peoples
> Are lessons the morals of which are followed by the just.
> I summarize all the books of the ancients

And recorded what they omitted.
I smoothed the methods of expression
As if they submitted to my will.
I swear I did not exaggerate
A bit; exaggeration is hateful to me.[11]

This ode, recited to his patron of the moment, is remarkable for several reasons. First, it has been noted that some of his present-day critics regard Ibn Khaldun as quite without morals. Yet if he is to be believed, while not striking an overtly moralistic tone in his writings, Ibn Khaldun is saying that when one does history honestly and portrays rulers who are acting in accord with the Sacred Law, history not only reveals moral standards but the writing of history itself becomes a moral act.[12] In this respect, it is interesting to compare this concept of the moral valence of scholarship with the later views of anthropologists who see their own work in much the same light.[13] Second, for all his obsequiousness, Ibn Khaldun does not bend the knee when it comes to his work as a historian: Whatever flattery he may have felt obliged to render in person to the rulers he served, he did not let it into his historical accounts. That, too, may be seen as a moral act.

Even during this period of relative isolation, the world of treachery and violence could still not fail to intrude. His father had retired from the world to pursue his own scholarship, but for whatever reason, the son was drawn back to it. As he says in the *Muqaddima*, "It should be known that it is difficult and impossible to escape (from official life) after once having been in it" (Ibn Khaldun 1969: 236). Whether because of illness, because he needed materials unavailable to him in his isolation, or because he missed the game, Ibn Khaldun reestablished his ties with the sultan in Tunisia. Once again he encountered the hostility and jealousy of other courtiers, for whom he undoubtedly had little patience (see Fromherz 2010: 86–87). However, when the sultan wanted him to participate in battles against rebel tribesmen, he sought to duck involvement by obtaining the ruler's permission to go on a pilgrimage to Mecca. In fact, Ibn Khaldun, now aged fifty-two, showed up in Cairo where his scholarly reputation preceded him.

Egypt at that time was ruled by the Mamluks, a dynasty largely governed by the manumitted slaves—often taken captive as children—used to staff its army and bureaucracy, a regime that was so graced with all the airs of civilized society that Ibn Khaldun could speak of "its scholars shining like moons and stars." Within two years he was appointed chief judge of the Maliki branch of Islamic law. But once again tragedy struck when his wife and daughters died in the sinking of the ship bringing them from Tunisia.[14] For the next fourteen years, Ibn Khaldun held various teaching posts, but his *Autobiography* contains few details

Figure 1.4. On the basis of fragmentary remains, Russian anthropologist Mikhail Garasimov recreated the appearance of Tamerlane. Photograph: Alexander Liskin, Sputnik. Available at https://sputnik mediabank.com/media/787185.html?context=list&list_sid=list _1003654.

Figure 1.5. Rembrandt based a drawing of the meeting of Ibn Khaldun and Tamerlane on an Indian portrayal.

about these years other than references to his finally making the pilgrimage to Mecca and a visit to Jerusalem in 1387. Throughout his time in Egypt, he was often criticized by opponents for his insistence on dressing in the North African style rather than in conformity with the style insisted upon by his Mamluk co-religionists.[15] While these years appear to have been relatively calm, one more notable adventure nevertheless awaited him.

In 1400–1, the great nomadic warrior Tamerlane (Timur), having previously conquered areas from Persia to southwest Asia, arrived with his army in Syria. Ibn Khaldun reluctantly joined his sultan who set out to meet Tamerlane in combat. However,

Figure 1.6. Tamerlane destroyed the city of Damascus notwithstanding the efforts of Ibn Khaldun to reach a peaceful takeover. Available at https://ballandalus.wordpress.com/2014/08/30/the-scholar-and-the-sultan-a-translation-of-the-historic-encounter-between-ibn-khaldun-and-timur/. Public domain.

learning of a threat to his rule back home, the sultan returned to Egypt leaving Ibn Khaldun behind. In hopes of convincing the Turco-Mongol conqueror to spare Damascus, Ibn Khaldun was lowered down the wall of the city at night to approach Tamerlane's camp. Knowing of the scholar's reputation, Tamerlane welcomed him into his presence. As Ibn Khaldun notes: "I entered the tent where he was sitting, inclining on his elbow, while the dishes were being carried before him to excite the appetite of the Mongol troops sitting in circles before his tent. When I entered I bowed and made signs of submission. He raised his head and extended his hand which I kissed. He ordered me to sit down and I did so where I was" (quoted in Enan 1979: 81–82). At once curious and fearful of the Mongol leader, he says to him at one point: "You are the supreme sovereign of the universe and the ruler of the world, and I do not believe that there has ever been a ruler like you among men from Adam until this era. Verily, I am not the type of individual who merely speaks about things based on conjecture." Having successfully pleaded with Tamerlane to spare the lives of the scholars of Damascus, Ibn Khaldun later writes to the sultan in Fez:

> I heard that their sultan Timur had asked about me, so I had no choice but to meet him. I went out from Damascus to him, and I was present in his council. He received me kindly, and I obtained from him amnesty for the people of Damascus. I remained with him thirty-five days, including mornings and evenings. He then dismissed me and bade me farewell under the most pleasant circumstances, and I returned to Cairo.[16]

Tamerlane requested that he prepare a full description of the regions with which Ibn Khaldun was most familiar, and over the course of the next six weeks he not only responded to Tamerlane's wish but "he explained to him some of his social theories about the vitality of the state and sovereignty" (Enan 1979: 82). Whether this included telling the great man that his Timurid dynasty was destined to fall seems doubtful. Indeed, there is some indication that Ibn Khaldun was prepared to consider Tamerlane's an exception to his interpretation of such regimes. The two men nevertheless shared a wide range of discussions, including Ibn Khaldun telling Tamerlane that drawing on his own higher state of Sufi perception contributed to his capacity to see history correctly (Fromherz 2010: 124). He clearly came to admire the conqueror, calling him "one of the greatest and mightiest of Kings." Unfortunately, the report he prepared for Tamerlane has not survived. Nor, in the event, did Tamerlane spare Damascus, and only a couple of years later, following his death, his empire collapsed under the weight of internal divisions.

Following his encounter with Tamerlane Ibn Khaldun returned to Cairo. There, as one court intrigue followed another, he was appointed and removed as Maliki chief judge no less than six times, until, on 16 March 1406, at the age of seventy-eight, Ibn Khaldun died.

*

To face such misfortune I turned toward patience,
But patience, itself impatient, abandoned me.
—Mohammed Ben Brahim Assarraj, "To al-Baghdadi,
the Pasha of Fez"

It is always tempting, in reconstructing another's biography, to succumb to hindsight bias, the tendency to perceive past events as having been more predictable than they were. In the case of Ibn Khaldun—from the tumultuous history of his ancestors to his losses from the great plague, his imprisonments, betrayals, and subjugation to the powerful—all of his experiences might lead one to explain his view of dynastic history as a story of witnessed decline and personal vulnerability. But while there is an inclination to reduce his experience to a Voltairean vision of history as "wooden clogs going up the stairs and silken slippers coming down," the truth is that Ibn Khaldun's choice of theories could not have been foretold from his personal history. For while his family background and education might have suggested he would adhere to the standard approach of his day to history as the story of great men and divine favor, instead he sought out connections wherever they might lead, relying on a radically rationalist method that led others—his friend al-Khatib most notably—into very deep waters and could easily have been read by Ibn Khaldun's enemies as granting a theologically impermissible level of control to humankind over its own fate. But ever tempering his rationalism with just that touch of mysticism and ambivalence so characteristic of his culture, Ibn Khaldun was able to walk a personal and intellectual middle path that fit well with his vision of the human career. His life and his theories share the common thread of searching out connections, an approach that has become an important part of the legacy he left anthropology.

Indeed, some commenters have suggested that Ibn Khaldun was less a historian than an anthropologist. And there are certainly features embedded in his intellectual biography that have become relevant to anthropological inquiries. The first is his exemplification of the role of participant/observer, a feature that bears more than a passing resemblance to the experience of the founding father of anthropological fieldwork, Bronislaw Malinowski. For just as Malinowski was forced into a fieldwork situation while incarcerated in the Trobriand Islands during World War I, so too Ibn Khaldun's interactions with the Berber tribes of North Africa was largely a function of the demands placed upon him by the sultans for whom he was constrained to work.[17] Like Malinowski, he made the most of the situation. In particular, he learned to treat his informants and the written accounts he consulted as personal repositories of information to be encountered and queried directly. In that he set a tone for research the product of which further legitimized the method. Thus as one returns to his work to ask how his analyses hold up or inspire further research one joins him in accepting the criteria he formulated for assessing the truth value of one's own research.

In terms of the intellectual history of anthropology, one might also say that Ibn Khaldun is somewhere between Thucydides and Marshall Sahlins, the former a supporter of history as propelled by human self-interest, the latter, arguing from a comparative ethnographic stance, the proponent of a more communal and indeed enchanted view of collective life (see Goodman 1972; Sahlins 2004, 2023). For Ibn Khaldun, the impetus for what (to borrow Sahlins's phrasing) "organizes rather than determines history" is the structuring of individual needs through collective cooperation to the point where habit becomes custom and custom becomes the engine for social solidarity. He is, in this regard, clearly moving toward a path of cultural analysis instead of a theory of the natural, the God-ordained, or the great man theory of history. His alternative to the comprehensive claims of cultural evolution or structuralism that have engulfed anthropology at various times is one that combines elements of the psychological, ecological, and organizational that has always been anthropology's unique contribution to disciplines that are too easily restricted to their own domains. To be reminded of the benefits of holism, that not everything is reducible to the political, and that (to borrow a phrasing) "for example is no proof" is to be reminded of the need to seek a very broad range of instances on which to base any theory.

Ibn Khaldun also was taught early on to rely on his own observations and not just those of others. The attraction of Aristotle's method of assessing causation fit well with his own experience, for he could readily see that simple reliance on those who claimed to possess the truth was not born out by either researched facts or common sense. But far from retreating to utter relativism Ibn Khaldun again found a middle course. Just as he could be obsequious when confronting power yet not permit self-preservation to color his account of history, so, too, he could find a middle course in doubting that which could not be confirmed firsthand. He may have gone too far on one occasion in wanting an opponent's books burned or in arguing that intellectuals always make poor rulers, but in each instance (as we shall see in chapter 6) he may have been confronting his culture's approach to ambiguity without reverting to simple determinism. If his solutions to these issues are not ours, his problematic and his quest are, and in that respect one can often find one's own path by seeing how another has carved his own.

Just as his teachers urged him to travel, Ibn Khaldun's peripatetic life surely impacted his thinking. He negotiated with Pedro the Cruel and Berber tribesmen, he encountered Muslims from the world over on the pilgrimage, and he studied ancient Greek philosophers. How open he was to other religions is unclear from his writings, but he pursued the example of Jewish history even though he does not speak of personal encounters with Jews and Christians or laud the Andalusian Convivencia that others have praised. He read extensively among Arab scholars but just how aware or affected he was by events elsewhere in the circum-Mediterranean is unclear. The fourteenth century was an incredibly tumultuous period in Europe, when famine, disease, incessant warfare, and financial crises sharply reduced populations and disrupted trade routes all the way out to India. Here, too, we have little mention of such events in his writings, but northern Africa was not isolated, and Ibn Khaldun, with his ear always close to the ground, is unlikely to have failed to notice that many of the same disruptions his part of the world was suffering were not unique. In particular, it is estimated that Tamerlane slaughtered 17 million people (5 percent of the world's population) in his conquests, and while Ibn Khaldun was certainly aware of Tamerlane's depredations—exacerbated by his own failure to get the conqueror to spare Damascus—one cannot help but wonder whether his prior experiences had desensitized him to some extent to the barbarities surrounding him or whether he simply felt he must treat the quantity of suffering he witnessed as secondary to understanding its structure.

Surely, too, his life experiences might account for what some commentors see as his tendency toward pessimism. It is not, however, a pessimism born of a view of humankind as inherently sinful or corrupt, nor of the course of dynasties as condemned to waste and degradation. Nor is it quite right to accuse him of fatalism, as B. A. Mojuetan (1981) does: Ibn Khaldun, as we will see, does not negate free will, and when accidents disrupt an existing pattern, he sees a form of renewal taking place instead of utter ruin. Rather, his is a rueful sense that unless people work at their own rationality, endeavor to free themselves from wrongheaded modes of understanding history, and fail to realize that the benefits of orderliness are paid in the currency of forgoing the pleasures of amour propre, the likelihood is that a new chance will arrive but only after the current one has been exhausted. Analyzing human psychology and human history in this relatively dim light nevertheless produced for him insights that might otherwise have been occulted by unwarranted optimism. Perhaps we should, therefore, console ourselves by saying of Ibn Khaldun, as Alistair Cooke said of Shakespeare, "you may learn more from his pessimism than from the optimism of lesser men." Perhaps he was, as Robert Irwin (2019: 208, 9) describes him, "a bleak and lonely figure"; "perhaps Ibn Khaldun did not expect the world to get any better and he had no hopes for the future." But many of his students and colleagues admired his vigor and found him excellent company. For example, Shams al-Din al-Sakhawi (1428–97) writes: "During Ibn Khaldun's retreats many people came to see him. He would welcome all warmly and put them at ease. He himself would frequent the halls of influential men and act humbly in their presence" (quoted in Himmich 2001: 17). Another said, "He was accompanied by many friends in his retired life; he was cheerful to them and often cut jokes with them" (Enan 1979: 103). Ibn Khaldun does, at least, seem reasonably optimistic about one thing, namely the enduring capacity of human beings to come together with a sense of communal solidarity. And it is to that engine of history—particularly as it relates to the rise and fall of dynasties—that we must therefore turn our attention.

NOTES

1. For more detail on his biography, see Alatas 2012; Dale 2015; Enan 1979; Fromherz 2010; F. 2000, and the translations of the *Autobiography*: Ibn Khaldun 1980 and 2006.
2. Dover (1952: 116–17) writes: "Ibn Khaldun is not more genealogically minded than his Arab contemporaries and predecessors: in fact, he is distressed by the pretenses of individual pedigrees and by the whole pseudo-science of genealogy. But such are his contradictions, he arranges a very handsome pedigree for himself! This blind spot is further emphasized by his belief that nobility is inseparable from asabiya." Enan (1979: 2–4) argues that there is reason to doubt the account rendered by the Andalusian genealogist Ibn Hazm (d. 1065) of the Khaldun family. Indeed, he says (Enan 1979: 4), "[t]here is reason . . . to wonder at the attachment of Ibn Khaldun to his Arab origin, for, in his Prolegomena, he shows strong antagonism and prejudice to the Arabs, while in another part of his history he praises the Berbers and extols their character and qualities."
3. On the role of the Khaldun family members in the travails of eleventh- and twelfth-century Andalusia, see Enan 1979: 6–7.
4. On Ibn Khaldun and Abili, see Nassar 1964.
5. Translation by Roger Allen in Himmich 2004: 69–70.
6. Quoted in Enan 1979: 20. A similar passage is rendered by Roger Allen (Himmich 2004: 67) as: "For what circumstance should I blame the nights, in what adversity wrestle with time? That I am far distant brings sorrow enough, removed as I am from the claims of my witnesses."
7. See, e.g., the hostile remarks made by the noted scholar Ibn Hajar al-Asqalani (2016), who lived from 1372 to1449, where he speaks of Ibn Khaldun's "tyrannical and iniquitous behavior" and says of his later

years in Cairo as a judge: "During this final tenure in office his conduct was characterized by excessive leniency, deficiency, and incapacity. . . . After being restored to office, Ibn Khaldūn resumed his usual conduct. He also expanded his residence on the shores of the Nile, would often indulge in listening to singing girls, spend his time with young men, and married a woman with a young brother of ill-repute. This led people to slander and defame him further." He also quotes another scholar of the day: "I read the following written in the handwriting of Jamāl al-Dīn al-Bishbīshī in his book *The Judges* (*al-Qudāt*): 'Despite all that he himself was engaged in, he was also notoriously scornful and disrespectful of other people.'"
8. We know little more about his wife other than that she was the daughter of a wealthy and renown Hafsid general. See Fromherz 2010: xi.
9. In his *Comprehensive Work on the History of Granada*, al-Khatib writes: "[Ibn Khaldun was] a man of virtue, combining all the finest qualities; highly esteemed and rock-solid in repute; revered in assemblies, high-minded and steadfast; exceptional in both the intellectual and narrative arts; many-faceted; a rigorous researcher, possessed of a prodigious memory, forthright in his concepts, skilled in penmanship, and wonderful company—in sum, a veritable paragon of the Maghrib region" (quoted in Himmich 2004: 17).
10. On their shared pessimism but different approaches to history, see Irwin 2019: 31–34.
11. Enan (1979: 56), who quotes this passage, notes that the ode was presented to the sultan Abul Abbas in 1382.
12. Akbar Ahmed (2005: 593) writes: "There is a moral imperative in his interpretation of *asabiyya* as the organizing principle of society. Muslims see human beings as having been created to implement the vision of God on earth through their behavior and organization of society: Man is after all a 'deputy' or 'vicegerent' of God ([Quran] Surah 2, Verse 30). So *asabiyya* as an organizing principle is not 'value free.'" Similarly, Hamilton A. R. Gibb ([1933] 1962: 173–74) writes: "Ibn Khaldun may be a 'pessimist' or 'determinist,' but his pessimism has a moral and religious, not a sociological basis." By comparison, Ernest Gellner (1975: 203) writes: "One of the interesting traits of Ibn Khaldun however is the extent to which he is a sociologist rather than a moralist. . . . [H]e indulges in no preaching. No advice is offered to the social cosmos as to how it should comport itself. Things are as they are. The thinker's job is to understand them, not to change them." Harvey Whitehouse (2024: 192–94) notes that while Ibn Khaldun indicates that uniting tribes and urbanites under one regime is a virtuous act since Islam is more likely to be followed in such circumstances, he also argues that it is a sacred duty

to bring heathens into the fold by citing the example of the commander who encountered people in India who engaged in practices forbidden by Islam and who were then properly killed, the heads of their leaders being publicly displayed.
13. See, e.g., Geertz 1968.
14. Ibn Khaldun's two sons survived, but we know almost nothing about them. His library was also lost in the shipwreck.
15. Doris Behrens-Abouseif (2023: 185) notes: "The fact that Sultan Qāytbāy, disguised in a Maghrebi outfit, went to pray at the Azhar Mosque to learn what people said about him, confirms that foreigners residing in Cairo maintained their national dress. Ibn Khaldūn is reported to have kept his Maghrebi dress even during his entire tenure as a judge in Cairo."
16. Ibn Khaldun 2014. Ibn Khaldun continues:

    This king Timur is one of the greatest and mightiest of kings. Some attribute to him knowledge, others consider him a Shi'ite because they note his preference for the members of the Ahl al-Bayt (family of the Prophet); still others attribute to him the employment of magic and sorcery, but in all this there is nothing but rumor. It is simply that he is highly intelligent and very perspicacious, addicted to debate and argumentation about what he knows and also about what he does not know. He is between sixty and seventy years old. His right knee is lame from an arrow which struck him while raiding in his youth, as he told me; therefore he dragged it when he went on short walks, but when he would go long distances men carried him with their hands. He is one who is favored by God—the power is God's, and He grants it to whom He chooses of his creatures.

    For further details see, Fischel 1952: 49-120.
17. I have not, however, noticed any indication that Ibn Khaldun spoke any of the Berber dialects.

CHAPTER 2

SOCIAL SOLIDARITY AND THE THEORY OF CYCLICAL HISTORY

• • •

Civilization flourishes or declines
according to the cohesion of its component parts.
—Ibn Khaldun, *Muqaddima*

The moons are protected from loss when they are crescents;
depletion reaches them once they are full.
—Abu Ali al-Hassan ibn Masud al-Yusi (1631–1691),
The Discourses

Suppose you were to describe a historical event—or even a long train of occurrences—relying mainly on your deepest assumptions about human nature and human relationships. If, for example, you grew up assuming that we are all conceived in sin and must rely on the strict instruction of those who understand the sacred texts to guide us away from our baser inclinations, how would your historical account be shaped? Imagine instead that you were to explain a leader's decisions in terms of his psychological relation to his mother or his policies as governed by the "invisible hand" of the marketplace: Would transferring theories from one domain to another appear convincing or misplaced? Would you employ analogies to make the unknown seem familiar or would you hesitate to do so, recalling Justice Benjamin Cardozo's warning that metaphors and analogies need "to be narrowly watched, for starting out as devices to liberate thought, they end often by enslaving it"?

Some of the most famous historians have made their mark by explicitly trying to form a theory of history based on a view of fundamental human nature. Others have not been completely open about such views and readers have ever since debated the implicit assumptions in their accounts. And then there are those who fall somewhere in between, historians who have a view of humanity and tell us how it bears on the course of events but who also seem to work with assumptions that for them are so obvious as to go unremarked. If earlier writers seem "modern" to us we may err in thinking that they must also share our background assumptions. But maybe we should let Ibn Khaldun speak for himself as he sets forth, in the opening passages of the *Prolegomenon* (Ibn Khaldun 1969: 5), his own take on these matters:

> History is a discipline widely cultivated among nations and races. It is eagerly sought after. The men in the street, the ordinary people, aspire to know it. Kings and leaders vie for it.
> Both the learned and the ignorant are able to understand it. For on the surface history is no more than information about political events, dynasties, and occurrences of the remote past, elegantly presented and spiced with proverbs. It serves to entertain large, crowded gatherings and brings to us an understanding of human affairs. It shows how changing conditions affected (human affairs), how certain dynasties came to occupy an ever wider space in the world, and how they settled the earth until they heard the call and their time was up.
> The inner meaning of history, on the other hand, involves speculation and an attempt to get at the truth, subtle explanation of the causes and origins of existing things, and deep knowledge of the how and why of events. History, therefore, is firmly rooted in philosophy. It deserves to be accounted a branch of it.[1]

If readers of the *Muqaddima* imagine that history is the domain of some professional elite rather than "the ordinary people,"

Ibn Khaldun, as we see, is quick to disabuse them. He scorns the writings of his predecessor historians, repeatedly calling them "stupid," the accounts they render "absurd," "silly statements" that are "more like the fiction of storytellers," whose "errors and assumptions . . . [prove that] blind trust in tradition is an inherited trait in human beings" (Ibn Khaldun 1969: 5, 14–15). Such historians, he argues, failed to confirm their sources, relied on misplaced analogies, and have shown "disregard for the fact that conditions within nations and races change with the change of periods and the passage of time" (Ibn Khaldun 1969: 24). While it may be appropriate in religious matters to inquire as to the reliability of the person transmitting knowledge—what is referred to as "personality criticism" (*al-jarḥ wa-t-ta'dīl*)—such a method "should not be resorted to until it has been ascertained whether a specific piece of information is in itself possible, or not" (Ibn Khaldun 1969: 38). Citing specific examples, Ibn Khaldun finds most historians at fault because they demonstrate (1) partisanship to a particular creed or opinion, (2) undue confidence in their sources, (3) failure to understand what was intended, (4) mistaken belief in the truth, (5) inability to place events in their real context, (6) desire to gain favor by praising those of high rank, and—most importantly—(7) ignorance of the laws governing the transformation of human society. He regards history as a branch of philosophy in the sense of it being amenable to rigorous scrutiny of cause and effect, and deeper history as being penetrated by application of knowledge gleaned from a variety of sources and approaches. Indeed it is in pursuit of those broader laws governing the rise and fall of dynasties that Ibn Khaldun fashions his methodology and his style of presentation.

Working with a basically Aristotelian concept of causality, Ibn Khaldun presents his theory as a logical set of propositions. Bringing each of these propositions into focus with telling examples and extending his theory to encompass domains that others had left unconnected, he unfolds his argument one step at a time, gathering his points as he proceeds, and seeking to convince by the sheer weight of his reasoning and relevant instances. He moves both synchronically and diachronically, at first setting out his view of the needs and propensities implanted in human nature, showing in turn how that nature is modified—if not indeed replaced—by the ways in which conduct and relationships become habituated, and then following the effects of social solidarity on the course of dynasties as they coalesce and fall apart. Blending detailed case-studies with movement along a structural timeline, he exemplifies not just a new way of thinking about deep causality but actually refashions the image of time. For whereas previous Arab historians related history as a series of snapshots of events and individual lives rather than as a chronological unfolding—an approach that is consistent with Arab visions of time to this day—Ibn Khaldun's quest for underlying causes and patterns leads him to a combination of chronology and structural accounting that is a major transformation in the way history had been told. Although he concentrates on structural factors there is also a story here, and it does no injustice to his style or argument to recapture his theory in such a fashion.[2]

Ibn Khaldun begins his story by setting forth the basis of human association. From our very beginnings, he says, human beings have had to depend on one another to fulfill their individual needs. Regardless of the form their society takes, all human groupings are affected by the physical environment in which they are situated. "Primitive" peoples, he says, can survive if the environment is not too harsh, but if they are so busy supplying their most basic needs they can develop neither their internal character nor their external system of social organization to a very high level. Like all people—whether it is those living as nomads, in settled groups of limited size, or in larger urban agglomerations—attitudes and practices tend to become so stabilized as habits as to recall Jean-Baptiste Lamarck's assertion that "habits form a second nature." Nomadic peoples may be virtuous for living simply, but their lives cannot nurture "the regimentation and hierarchical subordination which political rule necessitates" (1969: 195). Indeed, the form he refers to as "primitive" cooperation is one in which "there has first to be negotiation, and then partnership and such things as follow from it. Such dealings may, upon the combination of accidents, lead to disputes and contentions. Thus results discord, companionship, friendship, and enmity, leading to war and peace among nations and tribes" (Ibn Khaldun 1958: 2:68). Reliance on laws without a proper governmental structure or religion simply reinforces oppression; only a more developed form of "group solidarity" (*asabiya*) can bring the full benefits of civilization (Mufti 2009: 397). And it is this key concept of *'asabiya* that forms the next chapter in the story Ibn Khaldun has to tell.

'Asabiya can be translated in a variety of ways, depending on the extent to which the translator wishes to make it the precursor to terms now in use or seeks to portray it as distant from our own sociological vocabulary. Certainly the reverberations of any Arabic term cannot be ignored: As someone once quipped, every word in Arabic means something, its opposite, and one of the camel's delights. In Arabic, the root of any term (consisting of three or four consonants) forms what Edmund Wilson, speaking more generally about Semitic languages, called a "consonantal shell" from which a wide range of related meanings may be generated. So, for example, the root from which the term "Bedouin" is derived also yields "to be obvious," "to reveal," "to seem," "caprice," "ill-humor," "wilderness," "desert," and "whim." In the case of *'asabiya*, the root (*'-ṣ-b*) means to "wind, tie, or bind." From it one can derive words that refer to a "bandage" or the "winding of a turban," the forming of a "group" or the quality of being "high strung." In one form it can mean "solidarity," but in another "bigotry" or "fanaticism"; in one derivation it means "esprit de corps," while in another it implies "clannishness" and "racialism." What holds these meanings together is the sense of "binding," but whether in the positive sense of group solidarity or the negative sense of exclusivity and zealotry depends entirely on context. The term itself does not appear anywhere in the Quran, but it does appear over five hundred times in the *Muqaddima*. In fact, as Lars Gule (2014: 11) points out, in pre-Islamic literature *'asabiya* was used in a highly negative sense: "It was usually condemned as the blind support for the cause of one's own group, without regard for the justice of this cause. Therefore, *'asabiya* was seen as a manifestation of a pre-Islamic men-

tality. Ibn Khaldun was aware of this usage and condemns this form of 'asabiya."[3]

While Ibn Khaldun emphasized 'asabiya as a positive term, its translation into European languages has been quite varied. Robert Irwin (2019), Muhsin Mahdi ([1957] 1964: 196n1), and a number of writers translate 'asabiya as "social solidarity," while others (e.g., Rosenthal in Ibn Khaldun 1969: 26ff) employ such phrases as "group feeling," "esprit de corps," or "group loyalty." Yves Lacoste (1984: 102) argues that the concept applies only to specific hierarchically organized tribes rather than to social cohesion more generally, Albert Hourani (1991: 2, 449) characterizes it as "a corporate spirit oriented towards obtaining and keeping power," Al-Azmeh (interview 2021) refers to it as a "moral community" and "power group," and Abdesselam Cheddadi (1999) argues that since 'asabiya is necessary for the constraining force of authority, it is an indispensable aspect of claims to legitimacy.[4]

In the present study 'asabiya will be translated most often as "group solidarity," a phrase that has the benefit of being relatively neutral as to implied theories and appears close to Ibn Khaldun's various usages of the word. Defined in its simplest terms 'asabiya is that commonality with which a group of people, building directly or analogically on shared ties of kinship, guide the actions that, individually and collectively, serve their survival, their identity, and (under the right circumstances) their creation of a dynastic form of political organization. Put in this way, one can see that for Ibn Khaldun four things are true. First, solidarity is not a wholly independent variable. The degree of its cohesion—and hence much of its life course—depends on extraneous factors ranging from the role of religion in intensifying its possibilities to the environmental contexts that enable or restrict its development. Second, though 'asabiya displays characteristic qualities and depends for its structure and operation on forces that are largely invariant, accident plays a major role in whether it comes about or succeeds.[5] He refers to these as "celestial matters which man has no power to produce for himself" (quoted in Mufti 2009: 403). For example, climatic factors or—to choose the case he was most familiar with—the fortuitous outbreak of the bubonic plague will have a dramatic, even decisive, effect on the history of a particular group. So, too, in violent conflict: "Victory and superiority in war comes from luck and chance."[6] Moreover, leadership, as an indispensable aspect of group solidarity, comes up against the inevitable forces that structure dynastic histories, such that the relationship between the general and the particular, the structural and the idiosyncratic, the predictable and the uncertain must either be addressed or finessed if the theory is to hold up. Finally, *'asabiya* is as much a sensibility as it is a contributor to a resultant structure, and as such it partakes of elements that contemporary anthropologists would categorize as both cultural and social structural. Each of these orientations connects to the fundamentals upon which Ibn Khaldun's overarching theory of humankind and history depend.

Ibn Khaldun prefaces his story about the role of *'asabiya* in human history by noting that it has certain foundational premises, or antecedents (*muqaddimāt*)—features that sound eerily similar to what anthropologists much later referred to as "the functional prerequisites of a society."[7] Thus, human beings require a governmental form that responds to their psychological need for belonging, that secures them against want and chaos, and (under the right conditions) facilitates the development of those crafts and skills that Ibn Khaldun, following the ancient philosophers, refers to as "the sciences." *'Asabiya*, he says, has a very distinct nature that is generated out of everyday shared experiences. It is grounded in most instances in kinship, and whether the genealogy that a group shares is true or fabricated the idiom of blood constitutes one of the strongest contributors to group solidarity. As much as Arabs and Berbers may refer to their genealogies, Ibn Khaldun was, however, well aware that descent was frequently manipulated: He clearly states that *nasab* (kinship, linage, genealogy) "is a fictitious matter, it has no truth," "its function is association and solidification."[8] "A pedigree," he concludes, "is something imaginary and devoid of reality. Its usefulness consists only in the resulting connection and close contact" (Ibn Khaldun 1958: 1:265).

Indeed, as he is careful to note, kin ties may not be the only vehicle for creating solidary attachments. There is no simple correlation between organizational form and shared genealogy: Solidarity, for example, can be present or absent in any tribe. Moreover, common ancestry, even when strong, is not sufficient, for, as Mahdi ([1957] 1964: 197) notes, "the feeling of relatedness is dictated by the necessity of cooperation and self-defense." And as much as he admires the consociational aspects of tribal life—particularly among those who rallied to the Prophet's cause in the early years of Islam—Ibn Khaldun regards tribes as largely anarchic: "Whenever one tribe is destroyed," he writes (Ibn Khaldun 1969: 131), "another takes its place and is as refractory and rebellious as the former one had been"—an argument he documents throughout his *History* of the Berbers.[9] While the bonds that tribesmen form are particularly noteworthy, clients, religious followers, and even slaves—whether in a rural or urban setting—may form functionally equivalent ties.[10] But when urbanity and *'asabiya* coalesce a profound alteration may occur, leading in some instances to the formation of larger cultural and political units and thereby triggering the unavoidable life course of a dynasty. Although he does not believe that human history is governed by divine intervention or rigid laws of nature, for Ibn Khaldun social solidarity is not without its religious involvement. Indeed, he suggests, *'asabiya* must exist to carry out God's word, for only when there is a sufficiently high civilization, only when "the circle of justice" is intact, only when the oppression of disorder is set to rights can a society, a dynasty, have a chance, at least for a time, to flourish. It is at this point that the story picks up one of the vital keys to this development: the role of the leader. Here, Ibn Khaldun conjoins his vision of human nature and leadership into a single storyline.

In order to maintain a balance between human nature and an orderly society, he notes, one must start by recognizing that "each one will stretch out his hand for whatever he needs and (try simply) to take it, so injustice and aggressiveness are in the animal nature. The others, in turn, will try to prevent him from taking it, motivated by wrathfulness and spite and the strong human reaction when one's property is menaced. This causes dissension, which leads to hostilities, and hostilities lead to trouble and bloodshed and loss of life" (Ibn Khaldun 1969: 151–52). He continues: "People, thus, cannot persist in a state of anarchy and without a ruler who keeps them apart. Therefore, they need a person to restrain them. He is their ruler. As is required by human nature, he must be a forceful ruler, one who exercises authority" (Ibn Khaldun 1969: 152). He cannot come to this through mere descent for, as he rather drolly notes, "perfection is not passed on by inheritance" (Ibn Khaldun 1969: 307). To gain confidence in his ability to maintain order, the ruler, who like any man will have his latent aggressiveness "awakened by the scent of power" (Talbi 1973: 40), must at least project the illusion, through meekness and generosity, that he is in a mutually beneficial relationship with those who come to depend on him.[11] And therein lie various ambiguities.

On the one hand, 'asabiya is not simply the creation of a leader, while on the other his personal qualities and actions are all but indispensable to its florescence. Like the classic list of features that a caliph ought to possess, any leader should be knowledgeable, just, courageous in applying the law, and free of bodily and mental defects (Mahdi [1957] 1964: 242). With these, says Ibn Khaldun, a leader may legitimately exercise the power to dominate others, collect taxes, organize and carry out military ventures, and protect the borders (Ibn Khaldun 1958: 3:21). Indeed, it is important to note that Ibn Khaldun believed quite strongly in the hierarchical arrangement of society, where those of greater ability rightly ruled over those of less capacity. Nowhere does he suggest that 'asabiya equates with equality, the necessary control of human failings by a proper leader being indispensable to the vertical integration of a functioning society. In furtherance of that structure a legitimate ruler should gain his subjects' trust through his generosity, resist boasting of his power over others, and be ever vigilant in his relationships with appointees and subjects (Verza 2021: 122). He is indispensable to civilization, for "when civilization in the world has thus become a fact, people need someone to exercise a restraining influence and keep them apart, for aggressiveness and injustice are in the animal nature of man.... The person who exercises a restraining influence, therefore, must be one of themselves. He must dominate them and have power and authority over them, so that no one of them will be able to attack another. This is the meaning of royal authority."[12] The leader must, however, strike the proper balance: Too much force and "[his subjects] become fearful and depressed and seek to protect themselves against him through lies, ruses, and deceit"; too little and they cannot be kept apart when squabbling (Ibn Khaldun 1969: 153). Interestingly, Ibn Khaldun does not think leaders should be especially intelligent. Indeed, he argues that scholars make poor leaders: "Teachers," he says, "are weak, indigent, and rootless" (1969: 26). He continues: "[T]he Lawgiver [Muhammad] does not require excessive intelligence [in a ruler] ... for this may lead to oppression, misrule and the driving of the people beyond what they are accustomed to. . . . [I]ntelligence and foresight are defects in a politician, for they represent an excess of thought, just as stupidity is an excess of stolidity."[13]

Once ensconced in an urban setting the leader can avail himself of the fact that "[t]he submissiveness generally found in the human soul" helps to convert group feeling into dependence on the monarch. But in each moment, the leader must not stray too far: Ever the Aristotelian, Ibn Khaldun cautions the ruler that "[i]n the case of human qualities, the extremes are reprehensible, and the middle road is praiseworthy" (Ibn Khaldun 1969: 154). If "royal authority is the goal of group feeling" (Ibn Khaldun 1969: 109) and "likewise a goal of the perfecting details, namely, the personal qualities" of that leader, and if, further, "royal authority is transferred from one group to another—to the one that God permits to effect the change" (1969: 115), then the leader must simultaneously embrace the goodness of generosity and the metal of firm enforcement. As Bensalem Himmich (2004: 68), in his historical novel *The Polymath* has Ibn Khaldun say, "the ideal ruler is based on a combination of conditional generosity and outright violence."

Each feature of leadership thus carries within it certain contingencies and contradictions. The leader's role is contingent inasmuch as it continues to be subject to "accident." Stephen Frederic Dale (2006: 438), in discussing the "natural" course of a dynasty, thus notes that for Ibn Khaldun it is to some extent "accidental" whether a leader has been able to garner the necessary prestige to be effective and whether outcomes are crucially affected by climate, personal health, and similar factors lying beyond the inherent destiny of dynasties. If a ruler is to initiate or continue a dynasty "he will," as Mahdi ([1957] 1964: 256) phrases it, "have to possess the qualifications necessary for a leader and must be born in circumstances conducive to the creation of a powerful state, which in turn must follow the natural course of rise and decline." Referring to the early years of Islam, Ibn Khaldun (1969: 27) says that "[t]he men who controlled the group feeling now occupied themselves with directing the affairs of royal and governmental authority." Group feeling, therefore, is not alone sufficient: Leaders must arise who "control" it.[14] And though the course of *asabiya* in the history of a dynasty will not remain subject to one man's control there are mechanisms to be employed in its furtherance.

One can, for example, invent a genealogy to bolster the leader's alliances, even going so far as to link him to the Prophet Muhammad, notwithstanding that "all of these pretensions are nothing but flatteries by those [genealogists] who wish to please their rulers."[15] Such contrivances may, however, come at the risk of revealing a weakness: "Many leaders of tribes or groups are eager to acquire certain pedigrees.... They go after such a family and involve themselves in claims to belong to a branch of it. They do not realize that they thus bring suspicion upon themselves with regard to their leadership and nobility" (Ibn Khaldun 1969: 101). There is also some contradiction in Ibn Khaldun's theorizing in that the founders or rulers of a dynasty are said to impress their personal qualities and attitudes on the regime but are, at the same time, subject to forces beyond their control. He underscores the critical role of the individual when he says that a kin-based "house" may have a number of well-known and respected figures whose group feeling is attributable to the "nobility and prestige [that] are the result of (personal) qualities." Indeed, such nobility is not only "the secret of [group feeling]" but develops primarily from the margins of the existing power structure (Ibn

Khaldun 1969: 102, 105). But just as he always gravitates to the Aristotelian middle, here too Ibn Khaldun comments on a seeming contradiction when he suggests that apart from the merits of their way of life—a sense of honor, refined poetry, simple faith—there is "almost too much *'asabiyya* among the Berbers, too much tribalism and clannishness to form a long-lasting, authoritative state. . . . He writes in the *Muqaddimah* [Ibn Khaldun 2002: 452]: 'Every time a tribe is pacified, another takes its place, adopting the same attitude of rebellion'" (Fromherz 2010: 133). Playing upon the contingencies that accompany a dynasty's rise—yet always affected by the unavoidable forces that work on them—leaders must navigate between uncontrollable contingencies and potential contradictions in order to benefit from whatever *'asabiya* they have available.

Here, too, the forces of history follow a history of their own. For example, Ibn Khaldun notes that once a king achieves success he dispenses with *'asabiya*, replacing that sense of solidarity with the exercise of overlordship that rests on his control of surpluses rather than on the solidarity of real or fictive kinship. Indeed, dynastic history cycles through a series of stages (Ibn Khaldun 1969: 123–24). It begins when a solidary group, fueled by tribal attachment and not unaccustomed to plunder, establishes or invades a city. (Although he does not phrase it quite so, one suspects that Ibn Khaldun would have agreed with Marshall Sahlins's dictum [1968: 38] that "the town's wealth acts upon nomads as a magnet upon iron filings, not merely attracting them but bringing them together in the process." There is even a traditional Berber saying that "raiding is our agriculture.") In order to advance to greater civilization, the way warriors fight must itself become rationalized, with troops arrayed in proper lines and martial music encouraging a disciplined sense of shared purpose.[16] While still in their pre-urban mode, Bedouin, unlike sedentary populations, are not concerned with luxuries but only with the necessities of life, thus rendering them "closer to being good than sedentary people."[17] Recall that, when it came to discussions of the tribes, Ibn Khaldun spoke from extensive personal experience, whether from his occasional attempts to direct their energies toward a given regime or as an emissary sent to probe their weaknesses. Allen James Fromherz (2010: 88) cites from the *Autobiography* (Ibn Khaldun 2002: 157) a poem Ibn Khaldun wrote that captures his admiration for the tribesmen and their reciprocal relationship—here as it relates to an early caliph—to leaders generally:

> Amazing men, always in motion . . .
> Demigods, they have nothing but the desert mirage for drinking.
> And for their subsistence, a lance that they manipulate skillfully . . .
> But you have given them your favors, Thus they have given in to your power.

Matters change, however, when nomadic groups settle into urban areas. As the leader begins to monopolize surplus and indulge in a natural propensity toward ever greater control, the bond of kinship begins to be replaced by connections with impersonal subalterns—soldiers, bureaucrats, professional divines—who, though displaying a form of group feeling, themselves become habituated to obedience.[18] Dependence—indeed, humiliation—becomes routine since man "is not the product of his natural disposition and temperament." Ibn Khaldun can, for example, say of the Berber regimes in Spain that at the turning point in their cycle "they were enslaved by tyranny and had become fond of humiliation" (Ibn Khaldun 1969: 28). The balance between leadership as a guarantor of peace and leadership as undermining the individual's "fortitude" and self-regard may, at this juncture, become tilted since the inescapable truth is that man "is the child of the customs and the things he has become used to. . . . As a rule, man must by necessity be dominated by someone else" (Ibn Khaldun 1969: 95). It is at this stage, too, that the economics of a dynasty begin to shift dramatically.

"It should be known," Ibn Khaldun famously states, "that at the beginning of a dynasty, taxation yields a large revenue from small assessments. At the end of the dynasty, taxation yields a small revenue from large assessments" (Ibn Khaldun 1969: 230).

Early in the dynasty, urged on by the natural human propensity to gather resources and not yet having a full-blown taste for luxury and the habits that go with it, the ruler can keep taxes low and, so long as he is not in competition with his own followers, the religious law can continue to "legalize the use of cunning in trading" (Ibn Khaldun 1969: 242) without either personal humiliation or dynastic overreach. If, however, the monarch holds back from spending, events can spiral downward as the tax base decreases and incentive declines. "Dynasty and government serve as the world's marketplace," he says (Ibn Khaldun 1969: 23). Indeed, "the dynasty is the greatest market, the mother and base of all trade.... If government business slumps and the volume of trade is small, the dependent markets will naturally show the same symptoms, and to a greater degree" (Ibn Khaldun 1958: 2:102–3). As time goes by, collecting "the fruits of authority," the ruler actually begins to spend more and more, especially on luxuries. Although initially this engenders increased prosperity, enlivens the arts, and elaborates the network of the ruler's dependents (Ibn Khaldun 1969: 140), the scene is being set for inevitable decline, for "luxury wears out royal authority and overthrows it" (Ibn Khaldun 1969: 115). Taxes are raised to keep up the ruling elite's expenditures even as the economy is distorted by their demands: "Time gets the upper hand over the original group (in power). Their prowess disappears as a result of senility. [The duties imposed on trade by] the dynasty saps their energy. Time feasts on them, as their energy is exhausted by well-being and their vigor drained by the nature of their luxury" (Ibn Khaldun 1969: 114–15). At this stage, too, a shared level of complacency leads to the undermining of communal pride and exacerbates personal humiliation: Recall him saying of one such example that "[t]hey were enslaved by tyranny and had become fond of humiliation" (1969: 28). This in turn leads to increased demands on the supporting population, amplified fear of invasion, decline in birth rates, the eradication of incentives, the increase in cleverness over equitable dealings, and ultimately the withering away of the state—"like a dying out in the lamp whose oil is gone."[19] Just as in the life course of an organism—indeed, in Ibn Khaldun's view, of creation itself—so, too, every dynasty has an inevitable timeline, each of its stages requiring about a single generation, or some forty years, to play out.[20] In support of his thesis Ibn Khaldun offers a number of examples.

Indeed, it is in the examples of various dynasties that aspects of Ibn Khaldun's approach to social and political organization at large are most strikingly revealed. In his discussions about the earlier Berber tribal dynasties—the Almoravids (1050–1147) and the Almohads (1147–1215)—he deals with regimes that had traversed the entire cycle set forth in his paradigm. Of the Merinids (1215–1465), with whom he was a contemporary, Ibn Khaldun could claim to be witnessing a regime in the latter stages of its decline. Emphasizing that his schema is not necessarily applicable beyond the Berber regimes with which he is most concerned, Ibn Khaldun could, therefore, see in the Mamluks of Egypt (1250–1517) among whom he was living an example of a polity that may be displaying a different historical course.[21] It was in his account of the Mongols under Tamerlane that he thought he was witnessing a dynasty on the rise and, whether as cause or effect, his report of the encounter with Tamerlane may have colored his view of where on the cycle such a group might properly have been placed.[22] Although, as we have seen, he viewed such earthshaking events as the bubonic plague of his own day as utterly changing the world, he did not envision such events as eliminating the cycle of dynasties that was replicated in their wake. What he did do, quite aside from elucidating that cycle, was to make connections that, directly or not, reverberate through anthropology and the other social sciences to this day. Two of these, the concept of cohorts and the role of taxation in regime development, are especially noteworthy.

Central to the concept of *'asabiya* is the coterminous experience of its members. Their shared sense of solidarity, their involvement in common actions, and their joint projection onto a supernatural plane of the naturalness of their cohesion may result in a collective orientation that transcends generational differences. While he does not phrase it in quite this way, Ibn Khaldun appears to be working with a notion of cohorts that resonates with how later sociologists have employed that concept. Norman Ryder (1965), with whom the notion of cohorts is most identified, thus suggests that a particularly traumatic event may serve as a reference point for those who have experienced it at the same time, such that it constitutes a baseline against which they come to judge many of the subsequent events in their lives. This may firm up a generation's identity, but it may also unite people across generations. Examples would be the effect on Spaniards of different ages who shared the experience of the Civil War or, in the case of Ibn Khaldun's times, those who collectively survived the Black Death. Here, as for example in his comments about personal humiliation, Ibn Khaldun is well aware of the psychological effects of habituated behavior and accidental occurrence on the individual without losing that sense of how a community as a whole may be affected by a unifying experience.[23] Though parallel to rather than directly responsible for later sociological theories, Ibn Khaldun's implicit concept of the cohort is one with which later scholars can readily identify.

Of more direct influence is Ibn Khaldun's account of taxation. In the mid-1970s, the economist Arthur Laffer cited Ibn Khaldun in his argument that tax cuts would stimulate the economy whereas maintaining taxes at a high rate would produce the very economic decline to which Ibn Khaldun had pointed. To the Republican administrations of the era this validated their desire to cut the income tax rate, particularly at the high end. US President Ronald Reagan adopted Laffer's argument, citing Ibn Khaldun in the process.[24] However, the criticisms that have been raised about the Laffer Curve apply as well to Ibn Khaldun's original model: It fails to take into account a broad range of factors that affect the economy beyond tax rates alone, an increase in the economy may not generate as much revenue as a straightforward income tax, and real world examples show that supply side economics commonly lead to an increase in the federal debt, as was the case during the Reagan administration when the federal debt increased by two trillion dollars.

Perhaps the greatest impact for anthropologists of Ibn Khaldun's understanding of the relation of group solidarity to regime change has come through the writings of Ernest Gellner (1981: 202) who referred to him as "one of greatest thinkers—perhaps *the* greatest—in the social sciences." To understand Ibn Khaldun's appeal for Gellner it is well to keep in mind that Gellner was himself very attracted to large scale sociohistorical theorizing and asking how societies move from being decentralized to state-structured. He saw in the tribes of Morocco evidence of the capacity of large groupings based on common identity to organize themselves without recourse to a centralized authority, challenges to group solidarity being mediated when necessary by those saintly lineages who keep fractious behavior within bounds. As a Central European political philosopher, Gellner was, therefore, intrigued by that persistent question: How is anarchy possible? He also saw in Ibn Khaldun a precursor to Max Weber, characterizing the North African as "a superb inductive sociologist, a practitioner, long before the term was invented, of the method of ideal types."[25] Moreover, Gellner adopted elements of Ibn Khaldun's cyclical theory of dynastic history but argued that foraging, agrarian, and industrial societies achieve their version of *'asabiya* in different ways while still displaying the central importance of some version of solidarity that can do the work Ibn Khaldun ascribed to it. As one critic of his work noted, Gellner believed that all societies have a need for homogeneity.[26] Thus, the Ottoman Empire and modern industrial regimes have replaced the solidarity of kinship with that of various forms of nationalism. In a sense, then, Gellner sought to apply Ibn Khaldun's concept of *'asabiya* in ways its originator might have considered had he been looking at how societies have developed in the centuries following his own lifetime.

Akbar Ahmed (2002, 2005), who holds a chair in Ibn Khaldun's name, is another anthropologist who has paid tribute to Ibn Khaldun and extended that thinker's work into his own. He not only finds the concept of *'asabiya* relevant to contemporary problems in the Middle East and South Asia but sees in Ibn Khaldun's work a way out of some aspects of the current situation inasmuch as, avoiding the hyper-*'asabiya* of exclusionist groups, one can recognize the legitimate strength of group solidarity in many tribes and defer more substantially to their capacity to use their concepts of honor and organization to undermine the more extreme elements that populate the present political scene. Ahmed can, therefore, see in Ibn Khaldun's theories a way forward in the mutual understanding of cultures while still recognizing that one must add to Ibn Khaldun's work a more refined sense of just how the various aspects of social solidarity become operationalized.

A group of anthropologists at Oxford's Centre for the Study of Social Cohesion, under the direction of Harvey Whitehouse, have taken a highly interdisciplinary approach to group solidarity, arguing in particular that a combination of psychological tests and ethnographic field studies suggest that the cohesiveness that Ibn Khaldun spotlighted often arises out of shared experiences, particularly those associated with religious rituals. Their work proposes to fill a significant gap in Ibn Khaldun's work inasmuch as he does not discuss what mechanisms are indispensable to forming ʿasabiya through religion or why non-kin bonds, as the Oxford group argues, may serve as the functional equivalent to blood relationships.[27]

Gellner, Ahmed, and others who have been inspired by the *Muqaddima*, have, of course, been forced to contend with some of the lacunae in Ibn Khaldun's theory.[28] One may ask, for example, whether the success of the Berber regimes was due to group solidarity or to the brute force exercised by their most effective leaders.[29] Indeed, it is just as likely that since societies at war often experience an exhilarating sense of social cohesion it is not the kin-based, religion-fueled social solidarity that makes the rise of militaristic dynasties possible but the felt-sense of battlefield camaraderie.[30] The question of how group solidarity is actually formed and maintained therefore remains open. In *The Division of Labor in Society*, Emile Durkheim wrote: "The totality of beliefs and sentiments common to the average members of a society forms a determinate system with a life of its own. It can be termed the collective or creative consciousness." From Durkheim's perspective this consciousness somehow effervesces when a collectivity assembles, thereby making the whole of society greater than the sum of its individual parts. But by failing to specify the exact mechanisms at work that proposition only replaces one unknown with another. Or, staying with Durkheim, one could say that it is the similarity of roles that creates the mechanical social solidarity of more "primitive" societies, as opposed to those communities that achieve solidarity by assigning different roles to different persons in a way that mimics an organic body.[31] Yet here, too, the regression ends in uncertainty: Is the forging of social cohesion grounded in the universals of human psychology and biology, or is it particular to each culture? Ibn Khaldun incorporates elements of each of the several explanatory schemes without, however, specifying precisely the foundation of ʿasabiya. He argues that a leader arises out of a "necessity of existence" to bespeak the solidarity that may lie within his group, but he does not show exactly how credibility is achieved or how alliances are fashioned. He speaks of the tribes "who sought to favor war, source of their profits" without detailing the relation of that motivation to their baseline ʿasabiya. He gives examples of the rivalry of brothers and violence among cousins even within societies characterized by ʿasabiya without indicating how the strains of fission and fusion may actually coexist. He may, perhaps, have praised the tribes, as Fromherz (2010: 90, 162–63) suggests, in order to bolster his own credentials as a negotiator with them but he also glossed over the numerous instances in which tribes split into warring factions, thereby demonstrating that "blood is fluid even as it appears to be fixed" (2010: 161). Once again, for all his insights, Ibn Khaldun leaves the reader unsure if all the connections his logic counsels have in fact been adequately considered.

Other propositions raise similar concerns. Ibn Khaldun (1969: 246–47) argues that as a dynasty declines, "the group feeling that the ruler had through [its main supporters] is destroyed. It dissolves and its grip weakens," the group's place being taken by a set of retainers that "does not have anything like the powerful grip [of kin-based groups] because it lacks direct and close blood relationships." Now fear takes precedence over the prestige and command of language that previously held sway; now the felt-sense of belonging dissolves into personal agendas. But once again we are left unsure as to how the command of language and negotiating skills played out in the first place and, knowing how easily intrafamilial differences may dominate, precisely how alliances are forged even within the bounds of one's blood relatives. So, too, Charles Issawi (1950: 8) marks as a weakness in his work that Ibn Khaldun, while emphasizing that the societies he describes are not static and may be altered by accidents, only cites as a factor resulting in their change the contact they have with other societies, contacts Ibn Khaldun sees mainly as leading to destabilizing imitation and admixture. So, too, Ibn Khaldun's dichotomy between the urban and rural, settled and nomadic is not a sharp line. Many groups, we now know, move easily between both domains and in difficult times settled populations may leave their villages to re-engage a form of nomadism. To which "civilization" is one to ascribe those who are, in fact, comfortable moving between the two? Finally, on a more abstract level, it can be argued that *'asabiya* and its attendant concepts are not Weberian ideal types but assertions about actualities and as such they are trenchant descriptors of the Berber experience that may not always be sensitive to the full range of connections his method commends.

The works of various anthropologists who share Ibn Khaldun's concern with the dynamics of group cohesion also raise a series of fascinating questions. Marshall Sahlins and David Graeber argue that kings are imitations of gods, rather than gods of kings. Yet for Ibn Khaldun this would almost certainly not apply to his concept of kingship. He did not see kings as gods and nowhere in his work does one encounter the concept, so central to North African beliefs about saints, of *baraka*, that form of spiritual electricity that links those who possess it to the divine.[32] This may, of course, be little more than a definitional problem: The first caliphs may have been more in the category of paramount chiefdoms than kings in the evolutionary scheme Sahlins himself once embraced. But when even the first caliphs could not portray themselves as gods, when the ruler of the Almohad dynasty Ibn Tumart could not sustain a claim to be the Mahdi, and when Ibn Khaldun himself argues that prophets and Mahdis would still need to supply mundane proof of their claims then any challenger would be on an equal footing with rulers since all of them would be somewhat de-spiritualized, de-enchanted—and hence fungible—figures.

In each instance, the contributions Ibn Khaldun makes to anthropology often prefigure the approaches that subsequent anthropologists have taken as their own. Through most of the twentieth century, British anthropologists, as we have seen, eschewed history, whereas Ibn Khaldun shows the way to its incorporation within a functionalist paradigm. Indeed, his focus on the functionalist aspects of solidarity and its capacity to recruit individual loyalty compels consideration of the relationship of various parts of a sociocultural scheme that often escape notice when knowledge is confined to disciplinary silos. For all his emphasis on it, 'asabiya as some elusive force is not the end point for Ibn Khaldun's analysis of dynastic history. Rather it opens up a view of connections—economic, religious, legal, familial—that are also at the heart of the anthropological enterprise. The boundaries that he places around his study of the dynasties of North Africa belie any claims to universal explanation of all regimes. But his willingness to transgress the boundaries of prior scholarship is no less important for those social scientists who are willing, as he commends, to trust their insights, to situate their theorizing within the particulars of ethnographic detail, and to join him in recognizing that (to borrow the words of Amos Oz) "the more provincial you are, the more universal you get."

NOTES

1. Ibn Khaldun makes frequent reference to the importance of speculation in historical writing. "The [writing of history] ... requires a good speculative mind and thoroughness, which lead the historian to the truth and keep him from slips and errors." Previous historians, he says, "did not probe with the yardstick of philosophy, with the help of knowledge of the nature of things, or with the help of speculation and historical insight" (Ibn Khaldun 1969: 11).
2. Numerous commentors have retold Ibn Khaldun's basic theory, some by following his chapters in the *Muqaddima*, others by organizing their exposition in line with more contemporary issues. Among the most ac-

cessible overviews of what will be retold here, and upon which I draw, are Alatas 2013, al-Azmeh 1990, Dale 2015, Irwin 2019, and Mahdi (1957) 1964. See also the essays in Touati 2024, covering, among other topics, Ibn Khaldun's use of Aristotle, his approach to language, and his rational arguments concerning religion.
3. On the evils of *'asabiya* in the older sense of tribal loyalty at any cost see, the "Eighth Hadith: Prejudice *('Asabiyyah)*" by the Ayatollah Khomeini (1939).
4. See also, Cheddadi 2005. For a thoughtful set of comments on *'asabiya* see, McCorriston 2013.
5. "Every event . . . must inevitably possess a nature peculiar to its essence as well as to the accidental conditions that may attach themselves to it" (Ibn Khaldun 1969: 36). On the philosophical foundations of Ibn Khaldun's usage of accidental qualities (*a'rad*), see Dale 2015: 29.
6. Ibn Khaldun 1969: 229. He continues: "Victory in war as a rule is the result of imaginary psychological factors. . . . Trickery is one of the most useful things employed in warfare. It is the thing most likely to bring victory" (1969: 253).
7. On *Muqaddimāt* see, Dale 2006; on the concept of functional prerequisites see, Aberle et al. 1950. Bronislaw Malinowski's theory of needs also bears many similarities. See Piddington 1957.
8. Ibn Khaldun, *Kitab al-Ibar*, 6:138, cited in Hannoum 2021. See generally, Hamès 1987.
9. "[Ibn Khaldun] explicitly associated pastoral nomadic Arabs . . . with anarchy and chaos. . . . Tribal society . . . in political terms sometimes meant a virtual state of anarchy, thereby hardly deserving the name of an Aristotelian social organization, *ijtima'*, at all. He applied his derisive characterization to all tribes, except the very few that possessed sufficient social cohesion, military skills, and leadership to conquer cities, establish stable dynasties, and preside over prosperous, cultured societies" (Dale 2015: 28–29). Ibn Khaldun himself says: "No sedentary society existed among [the Berbers] long enough to reach any degree of perfection." Quoted from the *Muqaddima* in Dale 2015: 38.

It should also be noted that Ibn Khaldun passed quickly over the hoary question of the effects of the arrival of Arab tribesmen from the east into North Africa and whether those incursions fundamentally transformed or were incidental to the history of the Berbers of the region. Yves Lacoste (1984; "Ibn Khaldun and The Myth of 'Arab Invasion.'" *Verso*, 23 June 2017. Retrieved 7 March 2025 from https://www.versobooks.com/blogs/news/3293-ibn-khaldun-and-the-myth-of-arab-invasion) argues that these invasive tribes had less effect than other commenters have attributed to them and that even if Ibn Khaldun's binary divisions between nomad and settled, Berber and Arab were at times misplaced, his *History of the Berbers* clearly supports the proposition that "there is no historical basis for the theory that there was a basic antagonism between nomads and sedentary groups or between Arabs and Berbers. It is a myth . . . . The myth did not arise by chance. It was deliberately forged and inculcated into the framework of colonial ideology." On this point see also, Hannoum 2023.

10. "[O]nly those who share in a group feeling have basic and true nobility. When such people take people of another descent as followers, or when they take slaves and clients into servitude, and enter into close contact with them, . . . the clients and followers share in the group feeling of their masters and take it as if it were their own group feeling. By taking *their special place* within the group feeling, they participate *to some extent* in the descent to which that particular group feeling belongs" (Ibn Khaldun 1969: 103–4, italics added). Ibn Khaldun does not follow up in detail the words here italicized, so we are left without clear guidance as to the qualification he intends.

11. "The interest subjects have in their ruler is not interest in his person and body, for example, in his good figure, handsome face, large frame, wide knowledge, good handwriting, or acute mind. Their interest in him lies in his relation to them. Royal and governmental authority is something relative, a relationship between ruler and subjects" (Ibn Khaldun 1969: 152–53; see also Verza 2021: 121–31).

12. Ibn Khaldun 1969: 47. Elsewhere he writes: "I should like to know how long residence in a town can help (anyone to gain prestige), if he does not belong to a group that makes him feared and causes others to obey him" (1969: 103).

13. Quoted in Issawi 1950: 130. Nor does Ibn Khaldun really discuss the role of women as leaders, whether directly or behind the throne. The one exception are his remarks about the Kahina, the legendary seventh-century woman (reputedly Jewish) who led Berbers in their resistance to the Arab invasions. See generally, Hamli 2008, Hannoum 2001, and Hirschberg 1963.

14. In Akbar Ahmed's phrasing: Elders, chiefs, and prayer leaders "implement the notion of '*asabiya*" (New Wave History 2024).

15. Ibn Khaldun 1958: 1: 267–68. Here, too, one has an example of Ibn Khaldun's functionalism and confidence that the rationalism at the heart of his science of history can demystify such practices as the misuse of genealogies: "A pedigree is something imaginary and devoid of reality. Its usefulness consists only in the resulting connection and close contact. . . . 'Genealogy is something which is of no use to know and which it does no harm not to know.' This means that when common

descent is no longer clear and has become a matter of scientific knowledge, it can no longer move the imagination and is denied the affection caused by group feeling. It has become useless" (Ibn Khaldun 1969: 99).
16. Mufti 2009: 396. The discipline that a military leader exercises is analogized by Ibn Khaldun to the same guidance supplied by a Sufi shaykh, both of whom (including through music) play up that sense of attachment embraced in the concept of *wijdān*, which means not only "experience" but "passionate excitement," "psychic force," and "ecstasy". Mufti 2009: 406.
17. Ibn Khaldun 1969: 94. Perhaps the operative word in this quote is "closer" since Ibn Khaldun was not so complementary in his other remarks about the Bedouin. He writes: "because of their savagery, the Bedouin are the least willing of nations to subordinate themselves to each other, as they are rude, proud, ambitious, and eager to be the leaders" (1969: 94). What seems to transform them is religion: "But when there is religion [among them] through prophethood or sainthood, then they have some restraining influence in themselves." He continues: "The Bedouin are by nature remote from royal leadership. They obtain it once their nature has undergone a complete transformation under the influence of some religious colouring that wipes out all such (qualities) and causes the Bedouins to have a restraining influence on themselves and to keep people apart from each other" (1969: 120, 121). Before that, however, the Bedouin tribesmen can be ferocious: "They are among human beings what beasts of prey are among dumb animals... They do not stop at borders of their horizon. They swarm across distant zones and achieve superiority over faraway nations.... Places that succumb to [them] are quickly ruined." Cited from the *Muqaddima* in Mufti 2009: 389.
18. Of clients and *'asabiya*, Ibn Khaldun (1969: 98) says: "a client [-master] relationship leads to close contact exactly, or approximately in the same way, as does common descent."
19. Cited from the *Muqaddima* in Mahdi (1957) 1964: 209. Similarly: "At the end of a dynasty, there often also appears some [show of] power that gives the impression that the senility of the dynasty has been made to disappear. It lights up brilliantly just before it is extinguished, like a burning wick the flame of which leaps up brilliantly a moment before it goes out, giving the impression it is just starting to burn, when in fact it is going out" (Ibn Khaldun 1969: 246).
20. Ibn Khaldun (1969: 136) writes: "[A]s a rule no dynasty lasts beyond the lifespan of three generations." However, Rosenthal's note to this sentence states: "The following assumption of a period of forty years does not square with the remarks Ibn Khaldun makes here about the length of human life" (1969: 136n1).

21. On the Berber regimes see, Irwin 1997: 470–72; Ayalon 1980a, 1980b; and Van Steenbergen 2022. See generally Petry 2022. Ibn Khaldun also regarded the Ottomans as a potential exception to the pattern he found applicable to the Berber regimes. He characterized the Mamluks as having a "solidarity of convenience and clientage" (Himmich 2004: 118).
22. Ibn Khaldun saw in the rise of Tamerlane's line "a confirmation of his own theory of *'aṣabīya*, of group loyalty, or solidarity, on which, according to him, the continuity of a dynasty depended" (Fischel 1967: 103). He details the rise of the Mongols in volume 6 of the *Kitāb al-'Ibar*.
23. Toynbee (1954: 84–85) alludes to Ibn Khaldun's affinity with the concept of cohorts when he notes that Ibn Khaldun, in writing a history that looks at commonalities across regimes, effectively poses the question "What is this *Oikoumené* whose provinces—an Islamic World or an Iran or a Barbary—have discovered their kinship with one another through the common experience of a supreme calamity?"
24. Reagan 1993. The remarks by Reagan (including his mistaken assertion that Ibn Khaldun lived 1,200 years ago) can be viewed at https://www.youtube.com/watch?v=KETIOgYu5uc.
25. See generally, Gellner 1981 and 1988, Malešević 2022, and Skalník 2022.
26. Collini 2011. See also Martinez-Gros 2012.
27. See generally Whitehouse 2024: 192–94. However, Whitehouse's paradigm is at best imprecise and at worst formalizes several types of solidarity without actually specifying the mechanisms of their operation. His remarks about Ibn Khaldun's view of virtue and regime development may serve his own paradigm but misconstrues that of Ibn Khaldun himself.
28. See, for additional examples, Anderson 1984.
29. See generally, Bennison 2016. On the Almohads see, e.g., Dale 2015: 64–65. By comparison, Messier (2001) argues that the Almoravids never made the transition from a desert life to the city and their dynasty's collapse follows a somewhat different course than that laid out for them by Ibn Khaldun.
30. On the relation of these factors to Ibn Khaldun's view of holy war (*jihad*), particularly as it relates to the early Islamic period see, Mufti 2009.
31. On Durkheim and Ibn Khaldun see, Dale 2015: 280–83, Gellner 1975, and Turner 1971.
32. The idea of *baraka*, which does not appear in Ibn Khaldun's vocabulary, does not make its appearance in Moroccan discourse until the sixteenth century when the still-ruling dynasty of the Alawites merges it with claims of legitimacy based on descent from the Prophet to support their assertion of power.

CHAPTER 3

FREE WILL AND THE INDIVIDUAL IN HISTORY

● ● ●

> Man is the child of customs, not the child of his ancestors.
> Human actions control the whole world of things
> that come into being and all it contains.
> Everything is subservient to man and works for him.
> —Ibn Khaldun, *The Muqaddimah*

In comparison to his well-known cyclical theory of regimes, Ibn Khaldun's ideas about the relation of the impersonal forces of history and the exercise of individual choice rarely get adequate consideration. Although he did not address the issue with the same rigor he brought to his other inquiries, it may, however, be possible, starting with his views on leadership, human nature, spirituality, and uncertainty, to analyze more closely Ibn Khaldun's approach to the problem of the individual in history.

It is only in the most general and often rather indirect ways that Islam, in various sacred sources and popular beliefs, addresses the relation of individual actions and the forces governing the Community of Believers (*umma*). Although it stresses the God-given power of reason, Islam also recognizes that fate may prefigure, if not predetermine, an individual's decisions.[1] Nevertheless, Muslims tend to proceed as if they exercise control over their own actions, actions that are deeply connected to their place in society. A distinction, for example, is made between personal religious requirements (*ferḍ al-'ain*) and those religious duties some individual must perform on behalf of the community if it is to maintain coherence (*farḍ al-kifāya*), requirements that, like prayer itself, must be accompanied by the right intention (*nīya*). The Quran (Sura 35:18) states that "no man bears the burden of another," and five times each day intensely personalistic negotiations cease and all indicators of individual personality are submerged in the mass of indistinguishable believers. So, too, individuals may differ sharply in their viewpoints, but at the end of the day, as the result of unspecified forces or a useful fiction, the Prophet reassures his followers that "my community will not agree in error." Similarly, any leader who can consolidate his power is ipso facto legitimate, but if he leads the community as a whole into sin he may, in the eyes of most theologians, be removed by force. In the pilgrimage to Mecca the individuality of every person, wrapped in the winding cloth in which each will eventually be buried, is not only rendered virtually identical but men and women, who might otherwise be assiduously separated, are melded in the common ritual. And when, ultimately, the believer is arraigned on Judgment Day and the sins and good deeds of a lifetime are totaled, the prophet with whom one is aligned (Moses, Jesus, Muhammad) may step in to save the individual soul.

While such propositions as these offer a person with Ibn Khaldun's interests some general guidance, they do not constitute a coherent theory of the relation between historical forces and individual free will. Indeed, throughout his writings the relation of individual action and the historical forces that shape a governable community remain at once tense and unavoidable, problematic and unresolvable, borne along by the character of each person and confined by their surroundings. Particularly as it concerns the governance of the community the relation of individual freedom of action to the cyclical law of regimes remains integral to, if not always fully developed in, Ibn Khaldun's entire enterprise.

In one sense, of course, the role of individual action would seem to be overshadowed by Ibn Khaldun's other concerns. Consider, for example, his view of the relation of human nature to the course of history. Human nature he says, derives its particular features from the environment in which its participants are reared. Geography establishes limits and possibilities, internally by its effect on one's character and temperament, externally by how much one can or cannot control one's situation. Living a simple sedentary life may limit the complexity of one's existence at the cost of greater solidarity and creative actions, while nomadism may force negotiated ties and greater attentiveness owing to the competition among groups. Learning from experience and enacting that learning are not, in his view, simply a matter of one's race, for although Ibn Khaldun does at moments suggest that those living farther south are cannibals and not human he does not attribute any group's deficiencies to inherent traits but to the limitations their location places on their capacity to develop the features of a civilized society. He therefore castigates those who, following the Greek physician Galen, argue that the brains of Blacks are inferior to those of Whites.[2] Rather, he asserts, it is a combination of environment and lifeways that limit choice. He relates these factors to the issue of free will when, for example, as Muhsin Mahdi ([1957] 1964: 198) frames it, he argues that "kingship and solidarity have their origin in the animal faculties of man, and are not the product of voluntary choice only." He elaborates on this analysis when he brings together a series of factors relating to the Bedouin.

He begins, as he so often does, with background practices that become habits. Those groups, like the Bedouin, who abstain from rich foods and pleasure, he argues, tend to be more devout than well-to-do urbanites: "The reason or cause, *sabab*, for this is 'habit' (*'āda*) or custom that becomes part of a person's 'character' or 'nature,' his/her *jins* or *ṭabī'a*."[3] As they are bound together into groups for tasks essential to personal and collective well-being those who are closely related or whose solidarity (*'aṣabīya*) mimics that of close kin will find their cohesiveness is best reinforced by religion.[4] So placed, these solidary groups partake of the forces of history—the regularization of conduct by custom, submission for the greater good to a powerful ruler—that for a time assures a measure of stability. In the next turn of the cycle, however, solidarity is undermined by the weakening of common endeavor and the dissipation that accompanies much of urban life. At that point—when self-doubt and humiliation exacerbate the situation—a rival group, arising from similar sources as its predecessor, takes over. The forces of nature and the ineluctable cycle of dynastic life would, therefore, appear to trump most aspects of individual effort.

And yet there are, in Ibn Khaldun's view, countervailing forces, forces that would suggest not only a degree of free will but possible avenues for avoiding—or at least ameliorating—the demands of history and the human condition. Various scholars have noted some of these ways in which Ibn Khaldun implies a degree of individual choice informing the larger sociopolitical structure: "He believes in free competition and strongly condemns monopoly," notes Charles Issawi (1950: 16); God has created the capacity for intention and the acquisition of power, but, as Harry Wolfson (1959) points out, while for Ibn Khaldun mankind's lack of ultimate causal control is evident, just how extensive his limited control is remains beyond the student of history's need or ability to specify. As James Morris notes, Ibn Khaldun's many writings silently pass over the role of key actors,[5] debunk the idea of a Mahdi (a spiritual and temporal leader who will rule until the restoration of religion and justice), and do not comment on the transcendent power of saints.[6] Nevertheless, Ibn Khaldun prepares for Tamerlane a detailed report on the actions of some of history's greatest heroes.[7] His mixed approach to individual action even extends to the highest of religious figures, for in addition to emphasizing the standard Muslim belief that the Prophet is human rather than divine he says that even the Messiah will have to prove his personal leadership qualities.[8] Although, as we will see, it is possible to reconcile each of these seemingly conflicting positions, they present a challenge both to our understanding of Ibn Khaldun's overall view of human action and the logic by which he is able to sustain such potential contradictions.

Looking to his biography only heightens the uncertainty as to Ibn Khaldun's vision of the relation between individual acts and the cycle of regimes. Indeed, as we have seen, so much remains obscure in the life and thought of Ibn Khaldun that one commenter can flatly state that "little is known about the man."[9] Questions abound. Did he see the individual as carried along by the powerful personalities of his times or solely by the unavoidable currents of history and human nature? Having served numerous rulers, did he segregate their personal acts from the forces of which they were unaware, or did he maintain two contradictory propositions simultaneously either by separating the domains in which rulers affected him personally or by trumping momentary choices with a vision of their long-term irrelevance? Indeed, did he see his own efforts as so buried in the cycle of regimes that his withdrawal from the world to write the *Muqaddima* is best understood as prompted by a moment of submission to his own theory? If a certain form of double-mindedness was at work for him perhaps some of the insights of later social science may account for his approach.

Not uncommonly, anthropologists find that the relation of personal freedom and collective necessity is "solved"—or finessed—through a form of ritual inversion. A designated individual who stands between categories—a transexual, for example, or a saint—can open a path between the two in order to allow at least a temporary adjustment between social needs and personal proclivities. Alternatively, a ritual of reversal—as, for example, when the high-ranking are briefly rendered low and the low-born high—can simultaneously challenge and then recapitulate the status quo, creating at least the illusion of human control of the unpredictable. In the case of Ibn Khaldun, we know that he continually spoke of the internal and external aspects of things and that both were necessary for individuals to develop their capabilities to the greatest extent. As to the question of free will, we encounter what may appear as his curious inversion of the expected—in which free choice is said to be restricted to outward actions, whereas inward ones are beyond choice[10]—and see this inversion as a ritualized, internalized reversal of the normal, even if a sharp line between the two cannot be applied to every instance. Having withdrawn at least once from the world and congratulated his friend Ibn al-Khatib for proposing to do so permanently—only for his friend's freethinking religious views to lead to his being murdered by his intellectual and political opponents—was the ever-cautious, often dissimulating Ibn Khaldun trying to have it both ways by succumbing to the temptations of the ruler of the moment while professing there is choice in the world of historic forces even if there is only submission in the domain of the soul?

We can begin to sort through these often ambivalent and contradictory issues by concentrating on three domains: Ibn Khaldun's treatment of leadership, the relation of his Sufism to the question of free will, and his attitude toward that which can be known and that which, being relegated to the totally speculative, he regards as unworthy of further consideration.

Right at the outset there might seem to be an irreconcilable ambiguity in Ibn Khaldun's approach to leadership. Throughout his life he worked for, had intense conversations with, was appointed, reappointed, and jailed by strong leaders in various parts of North Africa. Some he clearly loathed, others (like Tamerlane) he clearly admired. He could, for example, say of the latter:

> The King Timur [Tamerlane] is one of the greatest and mightiest of Kings. Some attribute to him knowledge, others attribute to him heresy . . . still others attribute to him the employment of magic and sorcery, but in all this there is nothing; it is simply that he is highly intelligent and perspicacious, addicted to debate and argumentation about what he knows and also about what he does not know.[11]

Indeed, Ibn Khaldun saw a clear link between human nature and the need for strong leadership. Thus, he could say: "Now, the human species is one of the things the Creator has especially (enjoined us) to preserve. People, thus, cannot persist in a state of anarchy and without a ruler who keeps them apart. Therefore, they need a person to restrain them. He is their ruler. As is required by human nature, he must be a forceful ruler, one who exercises authority" (Ibn Khaldun 1969: 152). But what the relation is between that ruler's necessary qualities and the capacity he possesses to do other than what the course of dynastic history will prescribe for him remains less than totally clear.

If Ibn Khaldun thought—much less told—any of these powerful figures that they were simply being pushed around by forces beyond their control there is no indication that he did so. Indeed, in his own relations with rulers and adversaries he was constantly moving to advantage in ways he must surely have thought expressive of some degree of free choice. But whether one should see his self-confessed changes of allegiance as inconstancy or as the demands of the time does not solve the issue of the effect of personal actions on the unavoidable cycles of dynastic history. Ibn Khaldun may certainly have thought that even though the qualities of personal leadership had to be demonstrated through a leader's actions, he apparently believed that the end result of those leaders' actions would simply be part of a cycle beyond their control. These potential contradictions appear in a number of ways in his work.

Ibn Khaldun sees the personalities of rulers as crucial to the nature of their regime. Muhsin Mahdi, it will be recalled, notes that for Ibn Khaldun: "[T]he founder and the ruler [after him] create the regime and impress upon it their qualities and attitudes."[12] Indeed, as Ibn Khaldun himself notes, "the ruler's relationship to his subjects [is] one of possession": "Know, then, that the use of the ruler to his subjects lies not in his person, his fine figure or features, his wide knowledge, his excellent penmanship or the sharpness of his intellect, but solely in his relationship to them."[13] At the same time, as Stephen Dale (2006: 438) phrases it, "Ibn Khaldun identifies the 'prestige' of a given ruler as an accidental quality, by implication a necessary accident that evolves with each 'natural' stage of the dynasty." Ibn Khaldun also says: "Royal authority is the natural goal of group feeling. It results from group feeling, not by choice but through (inherent) necessity and the order of existence" (Ibn Khaldun 1969: 160). Several things flow from this approach. If, for example, an individual ruler, by dint of personal effort and understanding, is true to the Sacred Law (*shari'a*) then the worst effects of his rule may be avoided; if one makes a concerted effort to be in touch with one's inner spirituality even a ruler may hold at bay the less desirable effects of his actions. But there are clear limits: "Even when Ibn Khaldun describes tribal leaders who possessed superior *'asabiyah*, he attributes their success to social processes rather than individual brilliance" (Dale 2015: 195). The propulsion for dynastic cycles thus appears all but unavoidable. For even if some members of a society note that matters are going downhill, there is nothing they can do to stop the inevitable, any more than one can stop the decline into personal senescence.[14]

One factor that may reconcile these potentially conflicting images of the ruler's choices and the cycle of regimes is the absence in Ibn Khaldun's conceptual repertoire of institutions, in the sense of entities that exist separate from the individuals who occupy positions in them. Neither in the law, where the position of judge is inseparable from the person who is in that role, nor in the administration of the state, where the ruler cannot be expected to do something his office demands when he would be personally opposed to doing so, is it part of Ibn Khaldun's thinking that one might segregate the demands of a position from one's own preferred conduct. As a result, the intense personalism of Arab culture takes precedence over the establishment of a set of positions that could be unaffected by personal orientation. Stephen Dale concludes: "He [Ibn Khaldun], thus, remarks in an illuminating aside on government offices that he will discuss these positions, not to examine their legal status in Islamic law, but only to illustrate how they are generated—as accidents—by 'the nature of civilization and human existence' (*ṭabī'at al-'umrān wa-wujūd al-bashar*)."[15] If the *shari'a* were properly understood and applied it would constitute a brake on corrupt rulers, but since it is human beings who must apply it, the risk of misdirection is immanent. Ibn Khaldun's partial emphasis on personal presence even extends to prophecy: As James Winston Morris (2009: 266) notes, "One of his most significant remarks in this connection is his insistence (*Muqaddimah* 1:72–73) that prophecy does not exist by natural necessity but rather through religious laws whose efficacy and very existence depend above all on the persuasive powers of imagination in creating the politically indispensable supporting ground of popular belief and consensus."

Given this background scholars have taken equally strong, equally divergent positions on the issue of Ibn Khaldun's approach to free choice. Gaston Bouthoul is cited by Charles Issawi for the proposition "that the individual plays a negligible part in Ibn Khaldun's philosophy, since the individual's tastes and beliefs are conditioned by his environment and education and since the 'great men' of history have a minor influence on the course of events."[16] Issawi himself (1950: 7) concludes that for Ibn Khaldun "social phenomena seem to obey laws which, while not as absolute as those governing natural phenomena, are sufficiently constant to cause social events to follow regular, well-defined patterns and sequences . . . . [T]hese laws operate on masses and cannot be significantly influenced by isolated individuals."[17] There is, however, one other area in which his view of historic patterns and personal choice also enter into consideration.

The domain that may offer clues as to Ibn Khaldun's attitude toward free choice and historic constraint may be found in his thinking about Sufism.[18] As we will see more specifically in the next chapter, here the question of leadership and spiritual guidance collided in the rancorous (indeed, at times violent) disagreement among some of his contemporaries as to whether one must have a personal guide for such religious development or whether it was sufficient to learn from books what others have commended. While that issue may seem strange to our ears it is really a question of whether a personal attachment—like that of master/apprentice, teacher/disciple, patron/client, or debtor/creditor—carries with it that characteristically Arab cultural aspect of negotiated ties holding a society together and chaos (*fitna*) at bay.[19] Ibn Khaldun sided with the idea of having a master, rather than relying on written guides. In doing so, he not only appears to base credibility on assessing who is speaking and not just what they are saying but on being able to personally question another to probe for inconsistencies and truthfulness as opposed to a fixed and oracular voice that escapes interrogation. Here, then, the question goes beyond one of guidance alone to tap into the cultural bases for appraising truth by appraising the one who professes to hold the truth. As such, free choice enters in two key respects: in the choice of masters to follow and in using one's own reasoning powers to assess a person's credibility. Neither fate nor the cycles of history can do that work themselves.

Ibn Khaldun's approach to the relation of reason to spirituality also suggests how he may have segregated domains as part of his approach to free will and history. For him the rational and the spiritual are not in contradiction with one another. There is, he says, a hierarchy of knowledge—though it is not always clear where particular forms of knowledge fall on the ladder.[20] He acknowledged that some individuals possess a capacity to work alchemy, magic, and sorcery, that dreams can reflect reality, that one may be able to predict the future through the numbers that can be associated with the letters of the alphabet, that *jinn*s (the genies who live in the parallel netherworld described in the Quran) can influence human life, that divinely inspired deeds do exist, and when a Ouija board gave the answer he sought he literally danced for joy on the rooftop—all this while simultaneously asserting that such practices are not to be entirely trusted. Once again Ibn Khaldun's distinction between the internal and the external must be taken into consideration if we are to understand his vision of human choice. Thus, it is worth quoting what he says in his study of Sufism (Ibn Khaldun 2022: 13):

> Choice and human control determine external actions. Most actions of the interior are beyond choice, ungovernable, for control does not extend to the interior. Indeed, external actions operate subject to the control, direction, and choice of the interior. Thus, intention, which is the starting point of action according to the Law, is the origin—the soul—of all acts of worship. An action undertaken without intention is useless and cannot be considered part of a legally accountable believer's religious compliance. As the Prophet said, "Actions are judged by the intention that motivates them. Each person is recompensed based on intentions."

This passage might appear to be full of contradictions: To some Westerners, it may seem odd to consider internal thoughts as beyond choice yet to believe that overt acts can be accessed through the intentions that generate them—even as such intentions are somehow still subject to choice. Perhaps what reconciles these features in Ibn Khaldun's estimation could be phrased in the following way: Human beings are not the originators of their own passions. The quest for the necessities of life are promptings of our nature. But other elements of our interior life—the decision to place ourselves under the guidance of a knowledgeable teacher, the development of reasoning powers that allow us to govern our passions—are subject to our control over their overt expression. People who are completely incapable of forming a governable intention—children, for example, or the insane—cannot be held accountable for their deeds because they are unable to form the intention that can channel internal passions. Just as prayer is preceded by the statement of intention—effectively saying, "Lord, I am praying, not merely bowing down on the ground"—so, too, certain acts cannot be considered without their requisite intention being revealed by one's acts. There is a saying among contemporary Arabs that Ibn Khaldun would doubtless have recognized: "Marriage and cultivation occur only by intention." In other words, the law assumes that you would not engage in these acts but that you had the requisite intent to do the deed. As we will see later, this couples with a set of cultural assumptions that would appear to link Ibn Khaldun's day to that of his Arab successors. What needs to be underlined here is that the law presumes that marriages are valid and that people do not accidentally take over the land of others, thus bringing into the law presumptions based on a cultural postulate—one Ibn Khaldun articulates quite clearly—that it is indeed possible for people to make choices at some level, even though their animal nature accounts for the ungovernable urge to fulfill certain needs. Reason may enter at the margin to govern even those most basic passions so that excess and social harm to the community of believers may be contained.

Once again, Ibn Khaldun focuses on the key role played by a learned teacher. Indeed, he insists that Sufi acolytes cannot gain insight by mere participation in the devotees' rituals but must personally take responsibility for acquiring the qualities ideally associated with such adherence. Perhaps, like other Arabs, he could not imagine a self that is fragmented into a series of public roles, but he could imagine that normality may be turned on its head through lack of choice in the domain of inner spirituality. We are, therefore, once again confronted either by a theory of human willpower that is insufficiently thought out or one that is distinguishable by the domains in which it operates. This may explain why Muhsin Mahdi ([1957] 1964: 260) can conclude:

> Ibn Khaldûn's rejection of absolute necessity does not then mean that he refuses to give necessity a place in history, for that would have meant the reduction of all historical events to accidental events, i.e., to events that have no cause and, therefore, are unintelligible. Rather, he follows a middle course between two extreme and simple, though illusory, explanations: an explanation based on universal necessity and the negation of chance, and an explanation based on universal chance and the negation of necessity.

Finally, we may gain some insight into these issues by considering Ibn Khaldun's approach to uncertainty. At one level he appears to be quite certain: He believes there is a science of knowledge (though of questionable precision), he is confident that the *shari'a* is a practical law that can be applied with justice and consistency (as well as being readily susceptible to misuse), and he harbors no doubt that the capacity for spiritual self-knowledge has no prescribed bounds (even though individual acolytes will differ greatly in their spiritual development). He does, of course, distinguish among forms of human knowledge as, for example, when he insists that "the Prophet was sent to teach us the religious law, not medicine or any other ordinary matter" (quoted in Hourani 1991: 203). But like his approach to leadership and spirituality he places significant limitations on what can be known. He thus avoids specificity about the spiritual power of saints just as he avoids the hard questions about free will in the abstract. Indeed, he is very critical of mere philosophizing, and though it is unclear whether he places questions of free will in that category, it does appear that he was prepared to do so. We can see these ambivalences in his consideration of the work of various Muslim philosophers.

Favoring, but without great specificity, the Sunni position that God is the creator of all things, Ibn Khaldun was critical of those schools of thought like the Mut'azila who argued that God does not create all the acts of man, saying: "The Mut'azila, Rāfiḍīs, and Khārijīs arrogated worship and renunciation. Since their belief—and belief is always the root of all things—was distorted, their attempts to improve their deeds, whether inward or outward, were in vain" (see Özer 2017: 11). It is true that he was not unsympathetic to the work of Fakhr al-Dīn al-Rāzī (1149–1210 CE), who rejected the strict reading of both the Ash'arī and Mut'azila positions in favor of a rational reconciliation of philosophy and religious tradition.[21] Nevertheless, confronted with utterances like those of the Ash'arīs, who did not see man as a free agent but who clouded their own position by holding that such unfreedom only goes to the qualities (ḥal) of one's acts, or the position of the Mut'azila, who failed to clarify over which acts and to what degree God left choice to man—and notwithstanding his general support of Razi's viewpoint—Ibn Khaldun appears to have chosen to stand back to some degree from these disputes, perhaps because of their political and not solely theological implications.[22] In such philosophical contexts, where he believed that human reasoning had reached its limits, he simply concluded with the saying: *bi-lā-kayfa*, "which, freely translated, means, 'we know the contradiction can be reconciled, but ask us not how.'"[23]

There are, then, two possibilities that account for Ibn Khaldun's approach to individual choice and historic patterns: (a) That, notwithstanding their reasoning capacity, he really does not think that individuals operate mainly through their own choices and free will, or (b) that he is simply prevaricating. The former runs into problems (a) because he never invokes the forces of history as a reductionist explanation of his own actions, and (b) it is somewhat of a contradiction for him to be out in the world engaging in political acts if he truly believes they ultimately make no difference to the course of regimes. Either he thinks free will in the public domain is an illusion or he thinks that a well-educated man who understands himself can rise, however partially, above the constraints of background and history to effect change. Alternatively, Ibn Khaldun may have chosen not to concentrate much of his attention on the question of free will because (a) he categorized it, along with many other issues, as a pointless philosophical problem, (b) he saw it as "a problem we can go only so far in solving," and/or (c) he regarded the level at which causal explanation operates to be at a higher plane than that which would account for individual acts. That his writings do not supply definitive answers to these issues makes our own efforts to fathom his meaning all the more problematic.

Ultimately, one must conclude that Ibn Khaldun was less precise in addressing the will of the individual versus historical forces than he was in some of his other concepts. How representations within one's own thought processes lead to intentions that in turn lead to actions remains to Ibn Khaldun a mystery, just as the relation of God's power and mankind's freedom remain for him unresolved.[24] But is he to be faulted for this incomplete theorizing when neither religious nor philosophical thinkers have generated an unassailable vision of the relation of free will to the human condition? That his thinking on the question of human choice undercuts some of his theories about political organization and regime cycles does not mean that his insights about the forces with which any leader may have to contend are necessarily to be dismissed as well. Perhaps the final lesson for our own era is not that we are the pawns of history but that human reason— described by Ibn Khaldun to be like a balance meant for gold but sometimes misused for weighing mountains—must climb a wall of custom, habit, and potential constraints in the course of fashioning, both in public acts and in our spiritual lives, a regime of knowledge and individual will.

Ibn Khaldun is not alone in these matters. The issue of free will remains an intriguing if frustrating issue for anthropologists, even if it is only intermittently considered (Rosen 2024b).

When anthropologists began arguing that cultural relativity was not a vehicle for excusing any conduct whatsoever but a method of suspending judgment while trying to understand particular sociocultural systems, the problem of free will became an undercurrent that went largely unaddressed.[25] Philosophers and theologians, of course, have had their go at the problem of free will for centuries. Current theories come in multiple varieties. Determinism suggests that we are subject to laws of nature over which we possess no control and that prevent us from being the sources of our own actions. As a consequence, we can neither choose to do otherwise nor, in the view of some, can we be held morally responsible for our actions.[26] By contrast, those who argue that determinism need not be incompatible with choice share in the notion that the only criterion for free will is not the ability to do otherwise. Classical "compatibilists" thus argue that one is never fully blocked from doing what one wills; "modernists" argue that one may still be held blameworthy if one fails to apply one's reason to whatever range of possibilities nature presents.[27]

While philosophers continue to tangle over the theories of free will, psychologists, biologists, and neuroscientists have added their voices.[28] The results from these later disciplines have been as contentious as were those of their less scientifically disposed predecessors. We are told, for example, that psychological experiments demonstrate that those who believe they possess free will act more responsibly than those who do not share in this belief, or that brain scans and genetic research indicate clues to the mechanisms by which choice operates independently of cultural background.[29] Except for the diehard determinists, however, none of these investigations can claim to have chased both nature and culture into a corner and forced them to give up their previously well-hidden secrets.

It is unclear how Ibn Khaldun would have responded to the present approaches to free will. Perhaps, as we have noted, given his willingness to admit that certain issues remain beyond human knowledge he might have agreed with Isaac Bashevis Singer who quipped that "we must believe in free will, we have no choice." Successor anthropologists have either avoided the issue of free will or failed to resolve the contradictions in their own theories. Indeed, anthropologists—on the rare occasions when they have considered the matter more or less directly—have, notwithstanding a wide range of theoretical orientations, often seen human choice as severely restricted, if not wholly constrained, by one's cultural and social situation.[30] A century ago, in his effort to counter pernicious race theories, Franz Boas had said that "the behavior of an individual is determined . . . [by] his cultural environment."[31] Seeing each culture as an independent entity, the Boasians concentrated on mutual influences and unique designs but seldom addressed issues of choice. Proponents of the Sapir/Whorf hypothesis went further. To them, perceptions are so structured by the categories incorporated in one's language that members of a given culture cannot readily think and act otherwise than through the lens provided by that linguistic vehicle.[32] In Edward Sapir's own words: "The psychology of a language which, in one way or another, is imposed upon one because of factors beyond one's control, is very different from the psychology of a language which one accepts of one's free will. In a sense, every form of expression is imposed on one by social factors, one's own language above all. But it is the thought or illusion of freedom that is the important thing, not the fact of it."[33]

Other anthropologists, coming at issues from very different theoretical orientations, have been equally dismissive of free will. A materialist and evolutionist like Leslie White could argue that advances are brought about by changes in the ability of a society to capture more energy and to shelter and defend itself more effectively, such that any "science of culture" must recognize that "of this we may be sure: the alternatives to this view are free will and caprice, which are inadmissible as explanatory concepts in science."[34] Still other anthropologists have stressed that, since culture is primarily learned behavior, what a person is taught about his or her culture all but dictates the choices available,[35] or that the risks of cognitive dissonance severely limit the range of alternatives any member of a culture can sustain.[36] Indeed, the overall ethos of cultural relativism has, since the days of Franz Boas and his school, focused attention so sharply on the particularities of individual cultures that freedom of choice has largely been displaced by a discourse lacking any clear theory of the relation of cultural background to individual decision-making.[37] For all the contemporary talk about the "agency" of indigenous and subaltern peoples its purveyors have offered no explicit discussion about the age-old issues of cultural determinism and free will.[38]

Anthropologists on the European side of the Atlantic were no more specific. Through most of the twentieth century, British anthropologists, still fearful of relapsing into some form of social Darwinism and its political companion, a Whiggish view of history, also gave short shrift to free will. E. E. Evans-Pritchard spoke for many when, in discussing Azande oracles, he referred to "the fact that their intellectual ingenuity and experimental keenness are conditioned by patterns of ritual behaviour and mystical belief. Within the limits set by these patterns, they show great intelligence, but it cannot operate beyond these limits. Or, to put it another way: they reason excellently in the idiom of their beliefs, but they cannot reason outside, or against, their beliefs because they have no other idiom in which to express their thoughts."[39] Similarly, Raymond Firth argued that "structural forms set a precedent and provide a limitation to the range of alternatives possible—the arc within which seemingly free choice is exercisable is often very small." Firth tried to have it both ways, though, by referring to social structure as society's "continuity principle" and social organization as "allowing evaluation of situations and entry of individual choice."[40] So, too, the leading French anthropologists, ever under the influence of Cartesian dichotomies, largely favored a vision of culture as determinative of behavior. Thus for Claude Lévi-Strauss and his followers, the structure of the brain, organized around binary oppositions, prefigures the contrasts, molded and solidified through myth and ritual, that permit only a degree of bric-a-brac rearrangement, rather than meaningful alternatives, to the choices that can be enacted in any given culture.[41]

Ultimately, as we have seen, Ibn Khaldun does not address the issue of free will directly. Yet as one reads through his detailed accounts of the Berber tribes in the *Muqaddima* it is clear that tactical decisions are being made by individuals even if the broader pattern that results for the dynasties within which they are embedded would seem to have prefigured many of those choices. Along the way, however, more information that cuts across the domains of ecology, economics, social organization, and religious insight become grist for his interpretive mill—and hence our own. Ibn Khaldun has shown us what we must consider in such an endeavor, and that becomes increasingly clear as we next consider how his holistic view of history is deeply entwined with his views on religion.

NOTES

Epigraph: Ibn Khaldun 1969: 300, 335.

1. As this relates to Ibn Khaldun, see generally de Cillis 2017.
2. "Al-Mas'udi undertook to investigate the reason for the levity, excitability, and emotionalism in Negroes, and attempted to explain it. However, he did no better than to report, on the authority of Galen and Ya'qub b. Ishaq al-Kindi, that the reason is a weakness of their brains which results in a weakness of their intellect. This is an inconclusive and unproven statement" (Ibn Khaldun 1969: 64). A more forceful translation of this last sentence has been rendered as: "This explanation is worthless and proves nothing" (cited in Dover 1952: 113). On Ibn Khaldun's views on race, see generally Dover 1952 and Pišev 2019.
3. Dale 2006: 437, citing Ibn Khaldun 1958: 1:157–65.
4. "Social solidarity is found only in groups related by blood ties or by other ties which fulfill the same functions . . . .The clients and allies of a great nobleman often stand in the same relationship towards him as his kinsmen . . . . In fact, the ties of clientship are almost as powerful as those of blood" (Ibn Khaldun 1958: 1:235); "It is evident that men are by nature in contact with and tied to each other, even where kinship is absent . . . Such contact may produce a solidarity as powerful as that produced by kinship." (Ibn Khaldun 1958: 2:267). Presumably, then, these created ties must involve a degree of free choice, both by the central figure who fashions these ties and by those who choose one or another individual to whom they will be subservient.
5. Morris (2009: 277) suggests this is because Ibn Khaldun's readers would be familiar with these individual leaders:

    One of the most powerful (but also potentially most hidden) rhetorical methods in Ibn Khaldun's arsenal, which he uses constantly

in regard to contemporary Sufi writers, is his ability to pass over in complete silence key historical events, issues, actors, writings, and the like that his educated readers would surely know and that they would normally expect to be mentioned in a particular context.
Even if his contemporary readers did recognize what was left unsaid, the fact that it is personalities who tend to be downplayed means either that Ibn Khaldun thought their individual acts were irrelevant because they were simply the pawns of historic forces or that it was wise to be circumspect in referring to particular individuals whose adherents might still cause him trouble. Either way, the implication that personalities matter is still lurking in the background.

6. See Morris 2009: 255.
7. The exact content of the report he prepared within a few days for Tamerlane is not known: "We do not, and may never, know what this little book contained" (Mahdi [1957] 1964: 60). Referring to his *Autobiography*, Francis Robinson (2006) concludes: "According to Ibn Khaldun's account, they [he and Tamerlane] discussed . . . heroes in history." See generally, Fischel 1952. Enan (1979: 82) states that "He [Ibn Khaldun] also explained to him [Tamerlane] some of his social theories about the vitality of the state and sovereignty."
8. "The expected Messiah will not come to power automatically . . . . He will have to possess the qualifications necessary for a leader and must be born in circumstances conducive to the creation of a powerful state, which in turn must follow the natural course of rise and decline" (Mahdi [1957] 1964: 256). "He [the Mahdi] . . . must be one of them [his followers], and God must unite them in the intention to follow him. Any other way . . . without the support of group feeling and power, by merely relying on his relationship to the family of Muhammad . . . will not be feasible or successful." (Ibn Khaldun 1969: 257–59).
9. Özer 2017: ix. See also the introduction by Perez at Ibn Khaldun 1991.
10. "Outward actions are all subject to free choice and man's power, whereas most inward actions are not governed by free choice and rebel against human rule. The human rule has no control over the inward while the outward is liable to free choice, since it is governed by it and operates under its authority, command and instruction. That is why intention (*niyya*) is the principle (*mabda'*) of all actions, the foundation of (*aṣl*) and the spirit (*rūḥ*) behind all acts of worship" (Özer 2017: 9–10).
11. Quoted in Robinson 2006.
12. Mahdi [1957] 1964: 240, citing Ibn Khaldun 1958: 1:45:11.
13. Ibn Khaldun 1958: 1:341, in translation by Issawi 1950: 128–29.
14. "Once senility has afflicted a dynasty it cannot be reversed . . . . [S]enility is something natural in (the life of) the dynasty, it must develop in

the same way natural things come about, exactly as senility affects the temper of living beings" (Ibn Khaldun 1958: 2:117).
15. Id., citing Ibn Khaldun 1958, vol. 2: 3.
16. Bouthoul 1930: 27, quoted in Issawi 1950: 7.
17. Others are less clear on the matter. Fromherz (2010: 167), for example, says that "Ibn Khaldun's model of history only appears deterministic" because he describes the individual exploits of tribal leaders and others. But that does not address whether their acts ultimately fit a pattern over which they had no control. If free will means the ability to do otherwise just stating that matters "did not necessarily appear deterministic to those dynasties" hardly addresses the issue of free will proper.
18. Ibn Khaldun's writings on Sufism have been translated with commentary into English in Ibn Khaldun 2017, 2022, and Özer 2017.
19. See generally Rosen 1984. See also Rosen 2008: 121–30. For some commentors, the debate was based more on religion than philosophic rationality. See generally Meyerhof and Schacht 1937.
20. See Ahmad 2004.
21. Razi was the author of a thirty-two-volume exegesis of the Quran, *Tafsir al-Kabīr* (The great commentary), also known as *Mafātīh al-Ghayb*, and a manual of metaphysics, *Kitāb Muḥaṣṣal afkār al-mutaqaddimīn wa 'l-muta'akhkhirīn*. He wrote: "man is determined in the form of a free being" (*al-insān muḍṭar fī ṣūrat mukhtār*), a formula borrowed from Abu Hamid al-Ghazzālī (1058–1111 CE), who himself took it from Abu Ali al-Husayn Ibn Sina (Avicenna, 980–1037 CE) but interpreted it somewhat differently. For Ibn Khaldun's approach to Razi and these debates generally, see Gimaret 1980.
22. Razi was, after all, poisoned by his opponents, members of the Karrāmīya sect, much as Ibn Khaldun's friend Ibn al-Khatib had been murdered by his religious/political foes.
23. Wolfson 1959: 596. One is here reminded of Ludwig Wittgenstein's final statement in the *Tractatus Logico-Philosophicus*: "Whereof one cannot speak, thereof one must be silent."
24. See in greater detail the analysis of Ibn Khaldun's views on predestination in Wolfson (1959: 597) where the author concludes: "Perhaps in the age-old struggle between orthodoxy and rationalism in religion he saw nothing but a struggle between the suspension of reason and the perversion of reason and, like a goodly number of non-quibblers of every religion, he chose to suspend reason rather than pervert it."
25. Dorothy D. Lee's *Freedom and Culture* (1987) is such an example. In it the author equates freedom with being socialized to a given culture, rather than being offered acceptable alternatives to conflictual situa-

tions. Owing, perhaps, to the functionalism of her day, Lee does not join issue with the hard question whether freedom includes some significant range rather than some specific set of actions one is expected to employ in a given culture. See also, Bidney 1963 and 1995.
26. See, e.g., Waller 2011.
27. See generally, McKenna and Coates 2020.
28. See, e.g., Bartra 2014: 118–24; Tse 2013; and Harris 2012 (neuroscience "reveals you to be a biochemical puppet"). On philosophical discussions of free will, see generally O'Connor and Franklin 2019; Campbell et al. 2004; and Mele 2015.
29. See generally Sapolsky 2023.
30. For example, in his discussion of the use in a legal setting of the cultural defense, one author states that culture is not "a thing that can be entered or left out of one's own volition," his definition of culture including that it has "a decisive value or effect on the individual and society" (Berger 2021).
31. See generally, Boas 1945: chapter 2.
32. For an overview of anthropological studies of the relation of language to agency, see Ahearn 2010.
33. Sapir 1985: 112. Sapir goes on to say: "No two languages are ever sufficiently similar to be considered as representing the same social reality," and "Human beings do not live in the objective world alone, nor alone in the world of social activity as ordinarily understood, but are very much at the mercy of the particular language which has become the medium of expression for their society" (1985: 162).
34. H. White 1959: 174. White goes on to say:
    The notion that every human being is equipped with a conscience, a mechanism that can perceive and appreciate moral values in the external world, is old-fashioned and invalid. "Conscience" is merely the name we give to man's response to social stimulation in the ethical field. As Radcliffe-Brown has put it, "What is called conscience is thus in the widest sense the reflex in the individual of the sanctions of society." The "still small voice of conscience" is then merely a mandate of the tribe, making itself felt through the viscera and brains of an individual human organism (White 1955: 222).
    White makes a similar point when he writes: "How is [the] great variety of kinship nomenclature to be explained? Free will and caprice may be dismissed at the very outset" (1955: 131).
35. See, e.g., the testimony by John Hostetler in the Amish education case *Wisconsin v. Yoder* (406 U.S. 205 [1972]) as analyzed in Rosen 2018b: 227–46. See generally Rosen 2018b: 57–93.
36. See generally Berliner 2016 and Bae 2016.

37. For a brief overview of the positions and protagonists in this debate see, "Structure and Agency," *Wikipedia*, retrieved 7 March 2025 from https://en.wikipedia.org/wiki/Structure_and_agency. See also Geertz 1984.
38. For an annotated bibliography of works on agency, see High 2010.
39. Evans-Pritchard 1937: 337–38.
40. Firth (1951) 1963: 40. He calls social organization "the systematic ordering of social relations by acts of choice and decision."
41. This became a central concern of the students who took to the streets of Paris in 1968 castigating structuralism for its determinism and lauding Jean-Paul Sartre for his claim of free will. See Rosen 1971.

CHAPTER 4

THE ANTHROPOLOGY OF RELIGION
INNER STATES AND OVERT ACTS

• • •

> Our government makes no sense unless it is founded
> on a deeply felt religious faith—and I don't care what it is.
> —Dwight Eisenhower, Flag Day Speech, 1954

In a recent description of its offerings, one university stated that courses on the anthropology of religion are not aimed at establishing what is true in any given faith but are concerned with the overall role religion plays in society. That is not quite accurate. Depending, of course, on what qualifies, anthropologists do frequently concern themselves with the "truth" of religion, though not necessarily in the sense of "ultimate truth." To some, the truth is the consequence—the ability of a religion to give meaning and order to collective and personal existence—and in doing so to facilitate every form of human creativity from sacred music and architecture to poetry and dance. To others, truth lies in structure, whether by organizing groups to reflect the ineffable or through the rituals that conjoin individual feeling and the distribution of power. To still others the comparative study of religion can further enlighten everything from evolution and psychology to personal fulfillment and the human condition. In each of these ways the resonance with Ibn Khaldun's approach to religion as embracing and revealing certain truths is not as far removed from those of successor anthropologists as one might otherwise suppose. That Ibn Khaldun placed Islam at the focal point of his concerns should come as no surprise. But that he linked it to a broad range of political and historical forces, that he should have questioned the bases of successful prophecy or the rationality of the irrational only underscores his connection to later sociological and humanistic concerns.

At the core of Ibn Khaldun's approach to religion—as in his analysis of other features of human societies—are his many dualities: inner and outer, urban and rural, inherent and manifest, structure and event, essence and accident, particular and universal. Such distinctions may be seen either as entirely separate or indissolubly linked. Segregated, they cast light on their individual qualities; combined, they describe practical reality. And ever drawn to an Aristotelian middle path ("In the case of all human qualities, the extremes are reprehensible, and the middle road is praiseworthy"), Ibn Khaldun tempers his binaries with the admonition that they can be taken too far. Nowhere are these features and their constraints more apparent than in his axial concept of *'asabiya*.

On its surface *'asabiya* may, as we have seen, appear as the most secular of concepts: what could be more worldly than the way people, huddled together under a common rubric, carry out the ventures of their mundane lives? But Ibn Khaldun sees this unity—at least when it prompts collective ambition—as inseparable from its religious underpinnings. *'Asabiya*, he says, is the "secret divine agent" that binds such groupings together, reinforcing the common ties of kinship or circumstance. A strong leader may quash internal dissension in the absence of religious fervor or prophetic guidance—as the examples he cites from pagan groups and pre-Islamic times confirm—but it is religion that "restrains people from splitting up and abandoning each other. It is the source of unity and agreement, and the guarantor of the intentions and laws of Islam" (Ibn Khaldun 1969: 170). Indeed, he writes: "Religious propaganda gives a dynasty at its beginning another power in addition to that of the group feeling it possessed as the result of the number of its supporters ... [T]he reason for this is that religious colouring does away with mutual jealousy and envy among people who share in a group feeling, and causes concentration upon the truth" (1969: 126). It is a close question whether he would agree with a character in Barry Unsworth's novel *Losing Nelson* who says that "without authority there is no concept of the sacred." And his claim that jealousy and envy evaporate in the face of group feeling may be seen as either circular or pollyannish. But he would certainly agree that authority without religious support will produce neither the finest in human capabilities nor the justice and stability promised by the Sacred Law.

Although religion gives unparalleled vitality to *'asabiya*, it is interesting to note that for Ibn Khaldun sacred figures are assured of neither success nor legitimacy in the absence of demonstrated power. Indeed, in a sense one might think of them—like any other powerful figures—as having to prove their claims through worldly persuasion and demonstrated control: "The truth one must know is that no religious or political propaganda can be successful, unless power and group feeling ['*asabiya*] exist to support the religious and political aspirations and to defend them against those who reject them."[1] This is even true for the Mahdi as well as all the saints and prophets, for each of whom a kind of justification by acts is indispensable to the popular verification of their claims.

It is here, too, that one of Ibn Khaldun's dichotomies we have encountered before comes into play. In his book on Sufism, Ibn Khaldun repeatedly stresses that it is the formation of an interior state that accounts for resultant acts, that inner thoughts and needs feed back through habit to vitalize the propulsive force behind individual practice and collective well-being: "The Prophet . . . specified that internal actions are more important, because the interior is the source of rectitude . . . . In essence, what is desired from 'rectitude of the limbs' is the resultant effect upon the soul. When repeated over and over again, rectitude increases until right guidance takes possession of the soul" (Ibn Khaldun 2022: 9). "Sufism," he continues, "is maintaining the finest comportment in the sight of God in both interior and exterior actions, observing the limits ordained by God, prioritizing the inner workings of hearts and supervising their hidden dimensions, and thereby eagerly seeking salvation" (Ibn Khaldun 2022: 25). In the Quran, as noted, the second most frequently used word, after the name of God, is "knowledge." Ibn Khaldun elaborates: Such knowledge, he says, is not implanted complete in mankind even though "divinely imparted knowledge blossoms in the heart's inner recesses without any recognizable external catalyst" (Ibn Khaldun 2022: 39). When he came to write his treatise on Sufism he gave the book an intriguing title: "The Cure for One Who Asks, for the Improvement of Questions." In doing so he implied that understanding the ecstatic is both a test of one's own rationalism and the capacity of enthusiasm to enhance each individual's powers of reasoning and speculative insight. Once nurtured by wise teachers the result is the development of practical discernment. And yet, a significant degree of inchoate wonder remains, a wonder that is particularly evident in his approach to a wide range of "irrational" experiences.

Throughout, we have noted that caution is needed when assessing many of Ibn Khaldun's seeming lacunae and contradictions. If we make him solely a man of his own times we may miss his timeless contributions; if we judge him by the standards of a later era, we may dismiss him as premodern or seek to reconcile differences wholly in our own terms. We must begin with what he actually says about mystical experiences, both positive and negative. The list is impressive. He says that "the dead do have sensual perceptions," that a dead man "sees the persons who attend the burial and hears what they say, and he hears the tapping of their shoes when they forsake him" (Ibn Khaldun 1969: 357), that only a fool would deny that sorcery exists, that dreams may give foresight, that some people have the power of prediction, and that talismanic powers may inhere in the "letter magic" of a sacred text.[2] He employs the internal/external dichotomy when discussing some aspects of free will as they relate to these capabilities. Thus, he can say of the evil eye (Ibn Khaldun 1969: 395–96):

> The difference between it and the other psychic influences is that it appears (and acts) as something natural and innate.

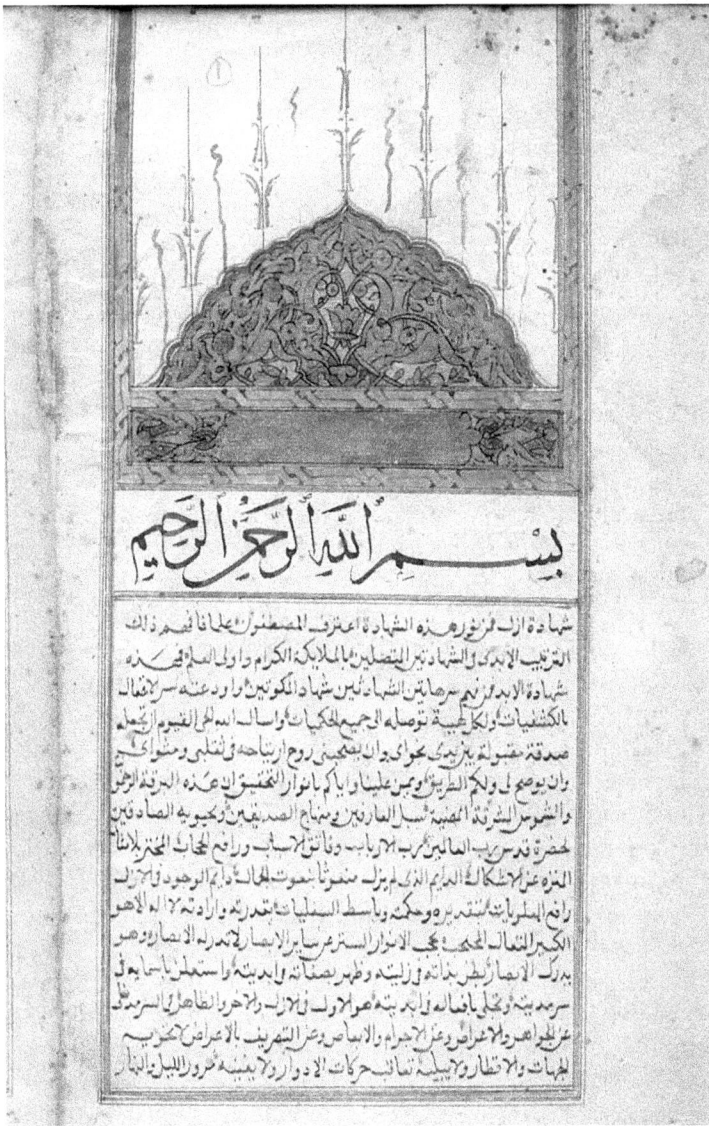

Figure 4.1. Manuals for the practice of magic were common in Ibn Khaldun's world, though he argued against their use in policy decisions. Wikimedia Commons, public domain.

It cannot be left alone. It does not depend on the free choice of its possessor. It is not acquired by him. Some of the other (psychic) influences may also not be acquired ones, but their appearance (in action) depends on the free choice of the person who exercises them. The thing that characterizers them as natural is their (possessors') potential ability to exercise them, not their (automatic) action.

If one were to take these assertions collectively and ask if they possess a common denominator two features would stand out: First, that Ibn Khaldun regards these modes of knowing as aspects of the interior state over which humans cannot exercise full control, and second, that even though these things exist they should not be relied upon to govern the actions undertaken by ordinary mortals and, most especially, their leaders. In other words, although inner states are not unrelated to the external world they cannot be trusted as guides to specific acts. Astrology may, therefore, be true, but rulers should not turn to it to guide their decisions; dreams may foretell events, but actions affecting relationships are more likely the result of larger forces, like the cyclical rise and fall of dynasties.[3] So, too, miracles may be wrought by the Prophet, but no one should claim them as justification for commonplace acts: "Miracles," he says, "cannot be used as analogies for ordinary affairs and constitute no argument against them" (Ibn Khaldun 1969: 255). Alchemy, on the other hand, is categorically denounced, not only for its frequent charlatanism but for the danger it poses to the economy (Ibn Khaldun 1969: 397–98). His discussion of these various practices is placed in the section of the *Muqaddima* on the hierarchy of sciences, thereby suggesting that they are subject to rational appraisal even if they are rejected as guides to action. Thus, in the treatise on Sufism that he wrote before the *Muqaddima*, he can draw his general point from one of his more telling examples when he says: "There is no denying the actual existence of all the sciences forbidden by the Law. Despite being forbidden, sorcery is real" (Ibn Khaldun 2022: 111).

Recall, too, that Ibn Khaldun spoke positively of Tamerlane's interest in magic and sorcery, but that he took this interest as an indication that the powerful man was addicted to intellectual discussion, not that he relied on such matters for his decision-making. So, too, he can repeat that "no intelligent person doubts the existence of sorcery . . . The Qur'an refers to it," but insist that its use is forbidden because it calls attention to beings other than God.[4] Characteristically, then, after this nod to theological necessity, Ibn Khaldun stresses the practical fact that charlatans deceive people into thinking they control these powers. One test of a wise ruler would therefore be his refusal to make decisions based on the claims of such sorcerers. It is in the same vein that he says dreams may be predictive but, since they may be the work of evil forces, dreams should not govern one's worldly affairs. Whether as a bow to convention, political self-preservation, or genuine belief, Ibn Khaldun places these mystical elements among the sciences for evaluation and strikes a somewhat Aristotelian middle course by acknowledging their reality but not their worthy application.

Comparison also plays a key role in his theorizing. Ibn Khaldun's reference to non-Islamic societies that have displayed the power of religion in fashioning their solidarity is only one of the ways he uses comparative religious examples to make his points. Throughout his travels, his reading, and his contacts with non-Muslims, he explored his general themes and tested his explanations.[5] He might, as a pragmatic functionalist, have accepted President Eisenhower's assertion that religion, rather than a select religion, is indispensable to a complex form of governance, but he also recognized that different religions carried different implications. In ancient Judaism, for example, he found support for his thesis that the stages of a dynasty's history are shared regardless of the particular faith involved. Specifically, he based his argument that it takes forty years for people to lose a sense of humiliation from the collapse of a former dynasty, a number he based on the period of wandering that characterized the Children of Israel after the expulsion from Egypt. He saw in the subsequent sedentary experience of the Jews evidence to support his thesis that such a way of life is integral to the development of civilization and new dynasties. His approach to these other faiths was, however, almost entirely historical and intellectual: He did not engage in debates about the relative merits of one religion or another—he was quite sure of the superiority of Islam (or at least was too crafty to risk indicating otherwise)—and though his reasons are unclear, he refused to enter the Church of the Holy Sepulchre during his visit to Jerusalem in May 1401.[6] Still, as Franz Rosenthal (1984: 24) notes:

> Religion for him is not restricted to Islam, although it took on peculiar forms in Islam. Its development toward sophistication and perfection is a rational process and subject to constant scrutiny. For a representative of the Islamic power structure such as Ibn Khaldun, and for anyone else in his time, it was apparently not within the ordinary and expected to rate religion in this way among the other aspects of life on an almost equal basis.

For all his rationalism Ibn Khaldun, like his co-religionists then and now, never employed doubt as a vehicle for acquiring

Figure 4.2. Jews and Muslims playing chess was an illustration of the relation between the two confessional communities in Spain and North Africa. Wikimedia Commons, public domain.

faith. He could be skeptical, certainly, of any number of dubious claims by historians or philosophers, but doubt about the fundamentals of Islam is, for whatever reason, never mentioned. As Franz Rosenthal (1984: 17) and many others have pointed out, "in the West, doubt . . . gained increasing currency and prestige" in the Middle Ages, whereas in Islam, doubt has long been equated with unbelief. There is essentially no equivalent of the proposition, heard from various sources in the West from the twelfth century onward, that "through doubting we come to inquiry, and through inquiry we perceive the truth." For Ibn Khaldun such an assertion in the domain of religion would be tantamount to a denial of the faith. Those who have tried to apply logic to the Almighty are in error, he says: Not only do they fail to grasp that "the intellect has nothing to do with religious law" derived from the Quran and hadith but he cites non-Muslim support when he concludes that "[t]he great philosopher Plato said that no certainty could be achieved with regard to the Divine" (Ibn Khaldun 1958: 3: 252) Indeed, were skepticism extended to Islam's foundational beliefs, Ibn Khaldun almost certainly would have argued that whatever social solidarity was in force would only be hastened toward chaos and civilization's demise.

Some commentators nevertheless have characterized Ibn Khaldun as a secularist if not indeed an "agnostic relativist." While it is, I believe, too much to suggest that "Ibn Khaldun is a product of Orientalism" in that he has been seen by such Westerners as a Marxist, a socialist, or an unrepentant materialist, the relation of his religious and historical orientation is better described by Bruce Lawrence (1983: 160) in the following way:

Ibn Khaldun was attempting neither value-free history nor a proto-phenomenology of religion. Yet his Islam was broader than the credal affirmations, the mythic reconstructions, the ritual requirements or even the judicial markings of his day permitted. Islam, to him, was the historical articulation of a divine plan that was rational and, therefore, could be interpreted by those who had eyes to see and patience to examine all that had been "revealed". . . . He was convinced there was a divine intent in history ... [and that] pursuit of the divine intention was a human responsibility.

As to his actual attachment to Sufism, matters are somewhat more complicated. Ibn Khaldun's intellectual interest in Sufism is clear, but was he an actual participant in the rituals—ecstatic or contemplative—of one or another Sufi brotherhood?[7] Here we have only a few bits of solid information. We know, for example, that he was buried in a cemetery associated with Sufis, but burials at such places were common and did not always imply significant participation in the organization.[8] Moreover, he was explicitly critical of the form of Sufism that predominated in his day. The "highly mysticised atmosphere prevailing in North Africa during his life" (Asatrian 2003: 77) was especially fervid during his years in Egypt, and the form of Isma'ili messianism that was prevalent

Figure 4.3. Notwithstanding his attachments to Sufism, it is unclear whether Ibn Khaldun frequented their prayer rituals. Wikimedia Commons, public domain.

appeared to him as particularly risky when it poured over into affairs of state. He does not doubt that some Sufi adherents may acquire insight beyond the ordinary: "Men who have followed Sufi training have, as is well known, as acts of divine grace, obtained perceptions of supernatural things" (Ibn Khaldun 1969: 84). He admired them, too, for a kind of Socratic "know thyself" quality: "Very few people share the self-scrutiny of the Sufis, for negligence in this respect is almost universal" (Ibn Khaldun 1969: 359). Noting the distinctive terminology Sufis developed and their tendency toward separateness, he can simultaneously acknowledge that "they perceive the realities of existence as no one else does" (Ibn Khaldun 1969: 361) and that Muslims of the Prophet's day, believing there was wider knowledge (especially of the Sacred Law) than the Sufis possessed, "forbade the discussion of those things and prevented their companions . . . from discussing the matter or from giving it the slightest consideration" (Ibn Khaldun 1969: 367). Those adepts who are not at the highest level "claim intuitive experience in connection with their perceptions and shun (rational) evidence. But intuitive experience is far removed from scientific perceptions and methods" (Ibn Khaldun 1969: 390). The real problem thus comes with the worldly implications of Sufism. James Winston Morris (2009: 254; original italics) summarizes the point: "[I]t is worth noting that the target of his criticism appears to be much less the truth and theoretical validity of the belief or activity in question . . . than what he implies are the *dangerous practical social and political effects* of such widespread popular beliefs in the society around him." After detailing Ibn Khaldun's reservations about Sufism, Morris (2009: 257) concludes:

> [I]t is not really the religious departure from the unreflective, active piety of the Companions [Sufi adepts] that he is criticizing . . . but rather (1) the much more practical and down-to-earth consequences of diverting substantial societal and human resources to the pointless, imaginary distractions and pastimes of such large groups of "simpletons"

as well as (2) the perhaps even more debilitating long-range consequences of their attempt to lead a moral and religious life that was somehow separate from what they allegedly viewed as the "corrupting" sphere of political and military power and authority.

It is also possible that some portion of Ibn Khaldun's involvement with Sufism was as much strategic as it was intellectual. In the highly contentious world in which he lived—where theological disputes could obscure the struggle for worldly power and factional alliances could rapidly turn into mortal divides—Ibn Khaldun may have combined orthodoxy and Sufism as he sought to maneuver carefully among the ever-changing political winds. To whatever extent it was true that Ibn Khaldun's approach to Sufism was carefully calculated, it is no less true that it was yet another domain in which he could emphasize the sociological implications of such attachments. At each point in his analysis he returns to the practical implications for the distribution of power in the state; at each juncture he recaptures how society, individual reason, and the organization of the sciences relate to one another. And in doing so he is cautious about taking sides when doing otherwise would compromise his basic orientation toward the practical. Still, he acknowledges enough of the claims he cannot wholly dismiss and charts a middle way that may, on more than one occasion, have kept him alive and well-employed.

Ibn Khaldun's middle course can also be seen in several other ways. Nowhere, for example, does he employ the phrase sometimes heard nowadays in the Maghreb: *lli ma'andush sheikh, shaitan huwa shaikhhu*—"he who lacks a Sufi master has Satan as his master." And while he appears to accept the common belief that saints are out of tune with this world but are responding to a different universe of experience, he is sufficiently skeptical of their worldly effects as to characterize even popular saints as "egregious failures."[9] It is, therefore, not surprising that scholars have come to quite different conclusions as to the nature and extent of Ibn Khaldun's attachment to Sufism and how it fits with his usual emphasis on rationalism. Revelation, he argued, teaches practical matters, whereas speculative philosophy is of no real value. Perhaps, as in the case of his thinking on free will and the forces of history, Ibn Khaldun's hierarchy of knowledge allows him to sustain without further speculation both a belief in the possibilities of irrational spirituality and a grasp of the knowable through one's God-given reason.[10] Sympathetic, perhaps, to those "authentic tidings of invisible things," as Wordsworth called them, Ibn Khaldun was prepared to address ambiguity where he saw it without feeling he must reduce all contradictions to utter certainty. As Fadlou Shehadi (1984: 270) notes: "In Ibn Khaldun's thought, the logical compatibility between scientific inquiry in one area and intuitive inquiry in another is reinforced by the cultural expectation that a place be found for the evidential-rational as well as the supra-rational intuitive and revelatory."

It is not difficult to see reverberations of Ibn Khaldun's thinking about religion in the later development of anthropological theory. He may lack a model of liminality (á la Victor Turner), an analysis of the connection between purity and danger (á la Mary Douglas), or a full-blown structural analysis of binary opposites (á la Claude Lévi-Strauss), but it is no stretch to appreciate that, unlike those who came before him, Ibn Khaldun created a functionalist approach to even the most sacred of religious figures and practices or that he saw in the capacity for inner discernment contributing to social solidarity a precursor to Emile Durkheim's ideas of effervescence and *conscience collective*. His linkage of the social to the economic could appeal to a Friedrich Engels, his focus on the relation between personal and collective religious experience could foreshadow the ideas of a William James, and his grasp of the materiality of the ineffable could coincide with a recognition that (to borrow Clifford Geertz's phrasing) "the *real* is as *imagined* as the *imaginary*." In each instance, Ibn Khaldun is, if not the father of these later concepts certainly their close relative, and in the details of his approach lie not only the elements of later disciplines but provocative ideas for ongoing consideration.

NOTES

1. Ibn Khaldun 1967: 258. He also says (Ibn Khaldun 1958: 1:324) that even "prophets in their religious propaganda depended on groups and families, though they were the ones who could have been supported by God with anything in existence, if He had wished, but in His wisdom He permitted matters to take their customary course." Morris (2009: 265–266; original italics) summarizes:

   Beliefs, opinions, and social norms serve above all to orient action and volition, both individually and collectively, and most of the discussions of Islamic subjects (including Sufism) throughout this book are meant to be understood from this very practical and clear-sighted perspective. As Ibn Khaldun illustrates at great length throughout the actual historical sections of his *Kitab al-'Ibar* (and not simply in the *Muqaddima*), such popular opinions vary greatly through history and various communities. What is politically essential about them is not whether they are true or false—categories that are properly applicable only to matters of reality subject to philosophical demonstration—but rather whether they are widely believed and followed and are therefore *practically effective* in assuring the common sociopolitical ends of human laws. One of his most significant remarks in this connection is his insistence [Ibn Khaldun 1958: 1:72–73] that prophecy does not exist by natural necessity but rather *through religious laws* whose efficacy and very existence depend above all on the persuasive powers of imagination in creating the politically indispensable supporting ground of popular belief and consensus.

2. For a comprehensive explication of Ibn Khaldun's approach to these occult sciences, see Asatrian 2003: passim. Irwin (2019: 60) argues that Ibn Khaldun was obsessed with predicting the future: "I believe that the chief reason Ibn Khaldun was so obsessed with sorcery was because it overlapped with divination and the power to know the future" (Irwin 2019: 128, see also 130). However, Irwin cites no direct evidence to support this statement.

3. One of the reasons Ibn Khaldun offers for his eagerness to meet Tamerlane concerned astrology. He writes: "The second reason why I have wanted to meet him relates to what I have heard from the astrologers and the Muslim saints in the Maghrib," and I mentioned what I have related before in this regard. [Interestingly, one of Timur's titles was *Sāhib-i Qirān* (the Lord of the Auspicious Conjunction), a reference to these astrological portents of his appearance]" (Ibn Khaldun 2014).

4. Ibn Khaldun 1969: 391–95. Interestingly, he barely discusses the place of the genies (sing. *jinn*), those creatures living in a parallel world who

occupy an important place in the Quran and whose existence a Believer cannot therefore deny. Thus, he finds the tenth-century historian and geographer al-Masudi's story about Alexander the Great and a many-headed sea monster incredible because "the jinn are not known to have specific forms and effigies. They are able to take on various forms. The story of the many heads they have is intended to indicate ugliness and frightfulness. It is not meant to be taken literally" (Ibn Khaldun 1969: 36). Perhaps, as in the case of astrology, Ibn Khaldun is saying that while the Quran may acknowledge that King Solomon could command the *jinns* reliance on stories about them as historically causal agents engaged by ordinary mortals in ordinary circumstances is not to be relied upon.

5. On Ibn Khaldun's comparative studies of non-Muslim religions, see generally Fischel 1967: 109–55.

6. "I abstained from entering the church . . . I refused to set my feet in that place." (cited from the *Autobiography* in Fromherz 2010: 72). On Ibn Khaldun's refusal to enter the Church of the Holy Sepulchre, Enan (1979: 79) quotes Ibn Khaldun saying: "This building raised by the Christian nations on the spot where Christ was supposed to be crucified did not appeal to me and I refused to enter it." It may be relevant that Muslims do not believe that Christ died on the cross but was taken directly up to heaven by God, hence Ibn Khaldun's objection may have been on these grounds rather than any anti-Christian sentiment as such. See also Fischel 1967: 136.

7. Morris (2009: 275–76) writes:

 An essential test of this interpretation of the relations of religion and philosophy in Ibn Khaldun's written critique of Sufism . . . is its congruity with what we know of the rest of his life and activity. And in fact, not only is there no sign of Sufi practice, study, or support in Ibn Khaldun's known career as a politician, court official, teacher, and Maliki judge (exemplified most notably in the outspokenly anti-Sufi fatwa with which we began), but the same sort of pointed, thinly veiled critique marks the beginning of his own autobiography, where the political failures and retreat of his own father and grandfather, after centuries of familial prestige and public renown, is suggestively traced to the influence of a leading Sufi preacher of Tunis.

8. Fromherz (2010: 111) says that "Ibn Khaldun died on March 17, 1406. He is buried at a Cairo Sufi cemetery; an appropriate burial for a man who practiced Sufism throughout his life and who often sought retreat from busy and seemingly fruitless political affairs" (2010: 111). Fromherz (2010: 153) further notes: "There have been repeated attempts to locate Ibn Khaldun's precise place of burial" by contemporary Arab

nationalists that have apparently proved unsuccessful. However, Fromherz's claim that Ibn Khaldun "practiced Sufism throughout his life" remains unsubstantiated.

9. Morris (2009: 247) notes:
> On a practical level, the essential human models, exemplars, and facilitators of this process of spiritual perfection are living, accessible, but most often immaterial mediator-figures (the root sense of *wali*) who either are no longer bodily in this physical world (as with the vast majority of the prophets and saints) or often are, even in their brief bodily time here, outwardly almost invisible or even egregious "failures" (as Ibn Khaldun frequently points out) if judged by the usual worldly criteria of social, intellectual or political accomplishment, nobility, and inheritance.

In a sense, Ibn Khaldun sees saints as reversals of the ordinary that prove the underlying rule: He "once more shows the non-social character of sainthood, since saintly knowledge ... does not enter into the divine economy of social well-being, and therefore a saint can be one who is unable to live a socially full life, being deprived of the pragmatic intellect" (Asatrian 2003: 89). By comparison, prophets are crucial to the operation of the mundane world: "There is a subtle distinction between the knowledge of a saint and a prophet. The knowledge of a prophet is superior to that of a saint because it is socially important" (Asatrian 2003: 83).

10. On Ibn Khaldun's argument that the Persian Sunni polymath al-Ghazali (d. 1111) made too sharp a distinction between knowledge of the outward (*fiqh al-ẓāhir*) and knowledge of the inward (*fiqh al-bāṭin*), see Özer 2017: xxxiv.

CHAPTER 5

SHARI'A, CUSTOM, AND THE ANTHROPOLOGY OF LAW

● ● ●

Blindly following ancient customs and traditions doesn't mean that the dead are alive but that the living are dead.
—Ibn Khaldun

Ibn Khaldun is rarely mentioned in discussions of Islamic law, even though he served as a judge on multiple occasions. With the exception of his writings on the management of court personnel his absence from such discussions is not entirely surprising (Gule 2015: 41). Treatises by Muslim scholars—as well as those by Western Orientalists—have long focused on normative and doctrinal matters. But these approaches were not Ibn Khaldun's forte, and as a result, neither he nor his supporters regarded him as a major contributor to Islamic legal theory (Dale 2015: 79). As a writer devoted as much to practical considerations as to the broad patterns of human history, he regrettably left little indication of how he handled specific cases.[1] Nevertheless, it may be possible, concentrating on his overall approach to cognate matters, to read between the lines and see how his approach to the law fit with his broader interests.

We have some information about his work as a judge. Over the course of more than forty-five years, Ibn Khaldun held various judicial posts. Most notably, he was appointed chief qadi of the Maliki school of Islamic law in Egypt six times, dismissed from that role five times, and ultimately died in 1406 during his last restoration to that office (Fischel 1967: 30–34, 39–41, 66–68). He readily admitted enjoying his judicial positions: As Franz Rosenthal (2000: 62) notes, "Above all he loved the power and influence of a judgeship," while a contemporary Egyptian historian, upon Ibn Khaldun's return to Egypt at the age of seventy-four following his encounter with Tamerlane, says of his quest for reinstatement as a judge: "May God have mercy upon him. How fond he was of office!" (Enan 1979: 87). Undoubtedly, many of his actions betrayed his unbridled ambition. As Rosenthal (2000: 47) further notes, in the eyes of some, "He was described as stern and correct when he was in office, and as obsequious to authorities when out of it."[2] Mohammed Talbi (1971: 828) reaches a similar judgment: "There is certainly no doubt that he behaved in a detached, self-interested, haughty, ambitious and equivocal manner."[3] He was even criticized for wearing Maghrebi clothing rather than that of the Egyptian qadis, proof, if one is to credit the remark of a contemporary, that he had a "love of being contrary in everything."[4] However, given the highly charged political environment within which he operated such assessments should be approached cautiously.

In particular, Ibn Khaldun was very concerned about corruption in the courts, and during his time as a chief judge in Egypt he did not hesitate to reveal the tactics of dishonest notaries and those providing advisory opinions (sing. *fatwa*) to the courts.[5] He said even of the learned men advising the law courts that they were constantly "mixing with princes . . . feigning to be just and therefore the princes considered them honest" (quoted in Enan 1979: 70). Seeing himself as a judicial administrator doing the best he could, rather than as a contributor to Islamic legal theory (Gule 2015: 41), he even went so far as to have some of these miscreants arrested and imprisoned.[6] In his *Autobiography* he details the corruption in the courts, saying of many lawyers and jurisconsults (sing. *mufti*) that they had "no experience studying with known scholars," finding inspiration only "in Satan."[7] But there is also some suggestion that, by being purposely difficult, Ibn Khaldun was trying to give himself some cover for attacking corruption, since doing so made it appear that opposition

Figure 5.1. Ibn Khaldun refused to dress like the judges of Mamluk Egypt. Available at https://bibliotecanatalie.com/f/de-medici-da-vinci-and-mamluk-sultan-qaitbay?blogcategory=Arab. Public domain.

Figure 5.2. In this document Ibn Khaldun's signature can be seen in the upper left-hand corner. Wikimedia Commons, public domain.

centered on his personality rather than an attempt to enhance his own power (Fromherz 2010: 86; Laabdi 2021: 33). Bearing in mind how his friend Ibn al-Khatib was killed by his opponents, any deflecting tactics Ibn Khaldun employed would not have been unreasonable. As he said of those who opposed his reforms, "Then enmity on every side increased and the atmosphere became dark between me and government officials."[8] Indeed, given the marked hauteur of his opponents one could imagine Ibn Khaldun saying of any of them, as does a character in Barry Unsworth's novel *The Song of Kings*, that "he was corrupt, and so more easily offended in his dignity than an honest man." Perhaps, too, Ibn Khaldun was not unmindful of the advice of his predecessor Abd al-Majid Ibn 'Abdun (c. 1050–1135) who had written:

> [The qadi] should not allow himself to be influenced and should avoid easy familiarity with the jurists ..., for harm can come to him from them ... [H]e should take care that none of them should show familiarity with him in word or deed, for this would lower him and diminish his orders and worsen his position. His judgment could be changed by someone's word or deed and the people would despise him. This would disturb the state of religion and disrupt the good order of this world and the next.[9]

Although primarily an administrator rather than noted scholar of the law, Ibn Khaldun did have extensive legal training.[10] Growing up in a well-to-do and well-connected family in Tunis he was educated in a wide range of topics, including natural philosophy, logic, mathematics, and metaphysics. He was particularly adept at the writing of legal documents and, having moved to Fez when barely twenty, he served an apprenticeship in judicial administration. Back in Fez several years later he said of his continuing studies: "I devoted myself to reflection and to study, and to sitting at the feet of the great teachers, those of the Maghrib as well as those of Spain, who were residing temporarily in Fez, and I benefited greatly from their teaching."[11] In his analysis of this background, Muhsin Mahdi ([1957] 1964: 73–84) suggests that the Maliki school of Islamic jurisprudence in which Ibn Khaldun was being trained, with its heavy emphasis on practicality, the "living tradition" of the Sacred Law, the role of evolving customs (rather than those of the Prophet's time and place alone), and interpretations based on a universal order that reason could comprehend, all had a formative effect on Ibn Khaldun's approach not only to law but to his broader study of history. The connecting point for many of these concerns was his overall method of analysis, a method that was influenced by both Muslim and European scholarship.

Over the course of his lifetime Ibn Khaldun became familiar with translations of the work of several Western philosophers, most notably Aristotle. Scholars disagree, however, as to the effect this had on his own thinking. To Muhsin Mahdi, Abdeslam Cheddadi, Aziz al-Azmeh, and Stephen Frederic Dale, Ibn Khaldun's theory of history is deeply dependent on the Aristotelian influence; to Taha Hussein, Robert Irwin, Claude Horrut, and others, failure to recognize the spiritual, even mystical, elements of his thought and reducing him to a secular sociologist misconstrues his distinctive orientation (Verza 2021: x–xi). Taking each of these interpretations into account three issues stand out.

First, as we have seen, Ibn Khaldun was interested in establishing causality on a firm basis of observable evidence. Like Aristotle he distinguished among various forms of causal explanation but clearly emphasized that which is effective in achieving a given end. Just as history could be seen only as a series of external events—one adventitious thing after another—or as having an internal order that has escaped notice by many historians, so, too, the law may be considered solely for its apparent "facts" or as possessing an inner structure and purpose influenced by reason, interpretation, and a realistic understanding of its integral relation to religion and society.[12] People will differ in their capacity to grasp causal relations, he argued, but unlike animals "the degree to which a human being is able to establish an orderly causal chain determines his degree of humanity" (Ibn Khaldun 1969: 335). Guided by a master, the student may transform the exercise of causal reckoning into a lifelong habit of analysis (Ibn

Khaldun 1969: 416–20). The specific skills that need to be developed are, moreover, essentially the same for both legal and historical analysis: insightful speculation (*naẓar*), critical investigation (*taḥqīq*), thorough understanding about the nature of entities and the causal principles by which they operate (*ta'līl li-l-kā'ināt wa-mabādi'ihā daqīq*), and in-depth knowledge of the modes and causes of events (*'ilm bi-kayfiyyāt al-waqā'i' wa-asbābihā 'amīq*). Through such terms as these it is also possible to see Ibn Khaldun's constant emphasis on the connections among disparate parts of a socio-cultural system.

For example, the Arabic word for "speculation" comes from a root (*n-ẓ-r*) meaning "sight," "surveillance," "discernment," or "attention." It also refers to an eye-shaped amulet that may serve as protection against the "evil eye." In the context of a method of historical analysis it implies that one who exercises informed contemplation may not only see the deeper structures that govern events but in doing so may cast up a level of protection against malevolence.[13] At the very outset of the *Muqaddima* Ibn Khaldun (1967: 11) stresses that "[t]he (writing of history) requires . . . a good speculative mind" and that without this quality, his predecessors "strayed from the truth and found themselves lost in the desert of baseless assumptions and errors." So, too, a thorough knowledge of the nature of different beings and events is as essential to ferreting out the truth in legal matters as in the patterns of history.

These are not, however, the only qualities that a judge must possess. Following the famous guidance for judges offered by the first successor to the Prophet, the caliph 'Umar, Ibn Khaldun cites favorably that figure's advice: "Use your brain about matters that perplex you and to which neither the Qur'an nor Sunnah [the words and acts of the Prophet] seem to apply. Study similar cases and evaluate the situation through analogy with them" (Ibn Khaldun 1969: 173). Logic, Ibn Khaldun says, has a place in the acknowledgment of religious truths, not because it is the vehicle for penetrating transcendental knowledge but because "it sharpens the mind in the orderly presentation of proofs and arguments." (Ibn Khaldun 1958: 3:257) Though he appears to regard at least certain fields of law—he mentions torts specifically—as best conducted by rulers with strong enforcement powers rather than being left to judges (Ibn Khaldun 1969: 174), he acknowledges (Ibn Khaldun 1969: 178) that it is the character of a judge, jurisconsult, or official witness (sing. *'adel*) that is most important.[14] Just as the credibility of something the Prophet reputedly said or did depends on the soundness of those persons who form the chain through which it has been transmitted so, too, the believability of an analogy or a preferred judicial approach depends on the capacity of a judge, by his reasoning or overall deportment, to convince others of the correctness of his opinion. And as we will see later, such assessments are themselves deeply rooted in those cultural assumptions about persons and actions that are integral to Arab culture generally.

It is also in his approach to law that Ibn Khaldun once again confronts the relation of the universal and the particular. For in legal cases, everything turns not only on the particular facts involved but on the general rules that must be applied across cases. Particularism shows itself in several intriguing ways in Ibn Khaldun's appraisal of the facts of a given case. Not only does he employ his method of tracing causation by seeking the consequences of acts, but he also focuses on individuals and their particular situation. One way we see this emphasis is in his advice that a judge or officer of the court should go out and encounter a person who has a case before him in order to observe that individual's behavior firsthand. This practice is consistent with the notion that people reveal themselves in the contexts of their interactions, and therefore their truthfulness, their reliability, their way of interacting with others will be more available to the trier of fact if he can see that individual, like a jewel turned in the light to reflect its multiple aspects, in diverse settings. Referring to Ibn Khaldun's comments on official witnesses (*'adul*), Kosei Morimoto (2002: 113) thus notes: "A candidate deemed suitable for the position can then serve as official witness for a judge, who can send him throughout the city to investigate the sincerity of litigants." Indeed, numerous Islamic law judges through the ages have been known to disguise themselves, go out into the market to encounter a litigant, and engage the person in a transaction similar to that in contention in order to discern the individual's honesty or customary practices.[15]

A second feature of Ibn Khaldun's approach to law concerns the relation of the *shari'a*, the Sacred Law of Islam, to the practicalities of everyday adjudication. In particular, Ibn Khaldun was confronted early on with the tension between granting primacy to the Sacred Law over reason or finding some means by which to reconcile them (Mahdi [1957] 1964: 27–37). For him, the religious law does not necessarily yield perfect application to mundane affairs. Not only is interpretation based on verses in the Quran and the behavioral examples set by the Prophet necessary to the proper application of the law but, he argued, one needs to consider divergent opinions and the customs of contemporary groups. Indeed, Ibn Khaldun saw the early years of Islam as ones in which divergence of opinion was vitalizing but that once the major schools of law had developed in the years after the Prophet's death such useful disagreement was limited to disputes within each school and was often far too abstract (Laabdi 2021: 52–59). Viewing the law of everyday adjudication as separable from the divine law, Ibn Khaldun could envision mundane law as thriving on conflict and change. Furthermore, Maliki law recognizes that insightful discretion (*istiḥsān*) may take precedence over the majority viewpoint and that decisions—many of which are collected as a form of case law (*'amal*)—may run counter to usual outcomes when one takes into consideration an overriding public interest (*istislaḥ*). This sense of practicality becomes manifest in numerous ways.

For example, Islamic law places great emphasis on the out-of-court resolution (*sulḥ*) of disputes, often employing a go-between (*wasīṭa*) or even a judge acting in his private capacity to fashion an agreement. It may seem curious, then, that Ibn Khaldun recommends that such resolutions should take place after a judicial decision has been handed down, whereas Maliki law commends settlements only if the judge cannot reach a final decision (Laabdi 2021: 32). The rationale here would seem to be that "bargaining in the shadow of the law" works best in Ibn Khaldun's schema if the law has first been applied and then is permitted to give way to an arrangement, often taking into account local norms, to which all parties have agreed. This concentration on the implantation of the law within societal norms, rather than as the embodiment of some abstract concept of natural or sacred law operating independent of social consequence, is particularly underscored by his treatment of local customary practice. Indeed, when an emphasis on custom is added to these orientations Ibn Khaldun's background in this form of sociological jurisprudence fits rather nicely with his approach to social history.

Custom is the unmarked category in Islamic law: It is not commonly listed—along with the Quran, the Traditions of the Prophet (*Sunnah*), consensus among the knowledgeable (*ijmā'*), and analogic reasoning (*qiyās*)—as one of the sources of law, yet it plays a key role even when so apparent as to go unacknowledged. One of the five leading legal maxims accepted by all schools of Islamic law itself states that "cultural usage shall have the weight of law" (*al-'addatu muḥakkamatun*).[16] Indeed, it often takes precedence over the other sources. In virtually every Muslim country and era, one encounters the proposition that custom (*'āda, 'urf,*) may take priority even over the *shari'a*. Ibn Khaldun might, therefore, have agreed with what has been said of the modern Bedouin, that "custom mostly provides the substance and *shari'a* its form."[17] He would also likely have agreed with Ayman Shabana (2010: 3), who notes:

> From the religious perspective, custom is perceived as a negative construct that corrupts the original and pure essence of religion. From the legal perspective (as a legal tool), on the other hand, custom is perceived positively as a means that enables the legal system to adapt and adjust to different contexts. By incorporating custom within the larger framework of legal theory, the jurists turned custom from a rival of shari'ah into a legal instrument that allows the legal tradition to adjust itself to different social and cultural settings.

Consistent with his views on the natural backdrop to human communities, Ibn Khaldun viewed custom as the embodiment of those habits that arise from ongoing practice. Indeed, "customs determine human nature and character": "Customs are like a second nature" (Ibn Khaldun 1969: 107 and 245). Moreover, he says, humans are born neutral as to good or evil, but "evil is the quality that is closest to man when he fails to improve his customs and when religion is not used as the model to improve him" (Ibn Khaldun 1969: 97). If, however, men become acclimatized to good customs—which is more likely if they live, like the Bedouin, in simple circumstances—they may move away from wrongdoing (Ibn Khaldun 1969: 94). Although Quranic references are at best allusive, some commentators, stressing the relation of the term for "custom" (*'urf*) and the cognate term for the "good" (*ma'ruf*) argue that custom can serve not just as a legal concept but as moral guidance (Shabana 2010: 45–58), and that a review of the authoritative Traditions demonstrates that "the concept of *'urf* permeates the entire landscape of the Sunnah of the Prophet."[18] To his striking assertion that "human actions control the whole world of things that come into being and all it contains. Everything is subservient to man and works for him" (Ibn Khaldun 1969: 335), Ibn Khaldun added: "[I]t is a fact that man is a child of ... customs .... He is not the product of his natural disposition and temperament" (Ibn Khaldun 1958: 1:258). Moreover, he says, "the condition of the world and of nations, their customs and sects, does not persist in the same form or in a constant manner," hence one must be careful not to project from one's own era onto events of the past (Ibn Khaldun 1958: 1:63). And while custom may aid continuity and address change (Shabana 2010: 12 and 124), as the quote from Ibn Khaldun that leads this chapter indicates, becoming static it may also hinder necessary alteration.

The third aspect of Ibn Khaldun's background that bears on the relation between his approach to law and his theory of history stems from his assertion that there is no contradiction between rigorous causal analysis and the importation of certain elements of the religiously "irrational." As a result of his training in law and philosophy he had to confront—and ultimately came to reject—the position most notably associated with Abu Hamid al-Ghazzālī (1058–1111) that mystical insight was separable from practical jurisprudence, such that an understanding of Ibn Khaldun's Sufism is as vital to understanding his approach to law as to his views on religion. Here, too, Ibn Khaldun's baseline proposition—that one can approach matters for both their internal and external aspects without either being given absolute priority and neither being inherently contradictory of the other—reinforces the need to consider that what may appear as contradictions in contemporary Western thought were not viewed as contradictions in his own day. The connection between law and mysticism appears in several ways.

In the previous chapter, it was noted that Ibn Khaldun's attitude toward Sufism is at times contradictory. In general, "the thing [he] dislikes most ... is the interference of religious idealism in the actual affairs of life" (Baali and Wardi 1981: 21) and, in the particular case of Ibn 'Arabi (1165–1240) whose Sufi writings he vilified in an advisory opinion (*fatwā*), he insisted that all of that author's works should be burned (Morris 2009: 249–50). Yet he respected the personal commitment of Sufi masters and sought in their style of contemplation insight into ways one might see connections not otherwise apparent (Ibn Khaldun 2022: 25 and 59). Indeed, when it comes to such practical matters as the law, it is tempting to think of Ibn Khaldun as a somewhat demystified, if not somewhat secularized, mystic (see Hannoum 2023), one who disagrees with the naïve (if not downright harmful) unworldliness of ecstatic belief but who retains a certain curiosity and regard for its discipline and suggestiveness. Certainly there is a similarity between the idea of education through a Sufi master and education of a future judge. And certainly, the fact that his denigration of astrology as an instrument of guidance for a ruler managed to sit alongside his curiosity about magic further suggests that his own line between the rational and irrational was not fixed. He rues the existence of too many books, since instruction should be personal and direct; he stresses the role of the individual, but he is not unmindful that losing oneself in the collectivity may bring moments of insight. And in each instance, his yearning, as judge and as historian, for whatever may yield practical results makes it somewhat difficult to pin him down on what furthers that end and what subverts it (see Mufti 2019).

As in his broader historical studies so, too, in his approach to law it is well to remember that Ibn Khaldun was very much a particularist. However much his universal history may suggest otherwise, he knew that the devil lay in the details. Thus, in addition to his concern with the methods of legal analysis and as an appellate judge reviewing decisions made by lower level judges (sing. *qadi*), in the Maliki courts Ibn Khaldun gave special attention to two legal domains in particular—bequests administered by the religious foundation (sing. *waqf*) and cases of disputed inheritance (Dale 2015: 100), both of which he worried over because of their vulnerability to manipulation and outright thievery by court personnel. Several factors make Ibn Khaldun's concern with charitable trusts and inheritance law especially relevant to our understanding of his general approach to society and culture. The Arabic terms for a pious bequest, rather like our term "mortmain" (the "dead hand" of a religious trust), imply a stoppage of normal exchange: *waqf* comes from a root meaning "to hold still" or "not let go," while the equivalent term used in North Africa, *ḥabus*, comes from a root meaning "to have custody, to confine or restrain." In one of the Traditions of the Prophet (*ḥadith*), we are told that "when a man dies all of his acts come to an end, except three: recurring charity, knowledge that benefits others, and a pious offspring who will pray for him." Similarly, "The Messenger of Allah said, 'O Abu Hurairah. Learn about the Inheritance and teach it, for it is half of knowledge, but it will be forgotten. This is the first thing that will be taken away from my nation.'"[19] How these features relate to Ibn Khaldun's larger project is particularly revealing.

Waqf endowments take property out of their normal role of creating relationships through the exchange of things. They freeze transactions in the interest of some stability and secure support for family members or a favored charity, but at the risk of bringing ongoing interactions to a standstill. That the terms describing inheritance and *waqf* are ones of fixity, restraint, and retention—which, as we will see later, run contrary to the image of men as needing to be mobile and adaptive—underscores Ibn Khaldun's belief that institutions may not only be corrupted by individual malfeasance but are poor substitutes for group solidarity and personal virtue. To then categorize charitable gifts as "recurrent" is to characterize them as of continuing import but at the cost of limiting further negotiation among affected parties. Moreover, while placing assets in a religious endowment technically keeps them out of the hands of the sovereign, it does not immunize such properties from the misdeeds of the ostensibly independent officials charged with overseeing the trust foundation. If these endowments are indeed subject to the machinations of corrupt overseers, the benefits of the trust and its claim of securing support for the beneficiaries will be lost and, in Ibn Khaldun's scheme, the decline of civilization hastened.

Inheritance, too, is a form of reversal of what is normally regarded as essential to the preservation of a community of believers, namely the constant engagement that is enlivened by the give-and-take of bargaining out one's relationships through material objects. For inheritance comes not by brokered engagement with others but by kin connections that are structurally independent of negotiation. There is, for example, no formal adoption in Islam and one can only designate one-third of an estate by will, the remainder being governed by the inheritance rules. Knowing the rules of inheritance is useful, then, not just because of its portent for future relationships but because the solidarity of groupings may be reinforced or fractured by the redistribution of wealth at death. So, too, the reference to forgetting the rules of inheritance in this regard is also revealing. The Arabic term for humankind is *al-insān*, "the forgetful ones," humans being seen as forgetful of what sacred text has revealed and thus at risk of descending into social chaos (*fitna*) and unbelief. Because the Prophet had suggested that the entire community of believers (*ummah*) might ultimately come apart and because the security of property protected by the religious foundation and rules of inheritance are susceptible to corruption, Ibn Khaldun's vision of social solidarity is highlighted by this point of vulnerability.[20] Both mortmain and inheritance are, therefore, crucial because they go to the heart of stabilizing a society in the maelstrom of political and factional infighting. Both have a deep effect on *'asabiya* inasmuch as they keep property away from the political arm and reinforce continuity in solidarity's most fundamental unit, the extended family. Perhaps that is why he was jealous to safeguard the *waqf* from corruption and to refer to inheritance law as a "noble discipline."[21]

Law, skeptics may say, is one thing, justice quite another. Yet in every legal system, whether as myth, ideal, or self-delusion, the quest for the one through the other remains vital, and hence the logic binding the two, while varying greatly across time and cultures, reveals much about other aspects of a cultural system. Absent the conditions in which good customs and religion can flourish, men, says Ibn Khaldun, will tend toward injustice, particularly in their disputes over property. He thus quotes the tenth-century poet al-Mutanabbi (915–965) saying: "Injustice is a human trait. If you find a moral man, there is some reason why he is not unjust" (Ibn Khaldun 1969: 97). Ibn Khaldun sees those groups that have achieved a high degree of solidarity as being more prone to avoid such injustice (Laabdi 2021: 40), but here the tensions and his recurrent skepticism remain pronounced. Those communities that become sedentary, he says, come to rely on secular laws—which are always expressions of power and always oppressive—whereas those educated to religious law are capable of greater self-restraint and fortitude.[22] Absent *'asabiya* people rely entirely on rulers, and even if those officials are relatively benign, any recourse to punishment "against someone who cannot defend himself generates in that person a feeling of humiliation that, no doubt, must break his fortitude" (Ibn Khaldun 1969: 96). Indeed, "injustice can be committed only by persons who cannot be touched, only by persons who have power and authority."[23] That is, one cannot have the same sort of equal position vis-à-vis a leader that one has with ordinary compatriots, with whom it is at least possible to work out a relationship employing a full array of personal connections and individual knowledge. As Ernest Gellner (1988: 239), not without a touch of his subject's own ironic sense, has said: "Ibn Khaldun's definition of government probably remains the best: it is an institution which prevents injustice other than such as it commits itself." Thus the assertion that "justice is a balance set up among mankind" (Ibn Khaldun 1969: 239)—which may seem rather anodyne—is actually deeply resonant within his own cultural scheme in that things must be capable of some equalization to be just whereas the differential of power between an ordinary person and a leader can seldom rectify the inherent imbalance in their positions. These propositions are then carried over into Ibn Khaldun's actual approach toward the application of the law.

In his *Autobiography* Ibn Khaldun says: "I considered the plaintiff and the accused equally, without any concern for their status or power in society; I gave assistance to any weaker party, to level out power inequalities; I refused mediation or petitions on either party's behalf. I focused on finding the truth only by attending to the evidence."[24] There are two intriguing elements to this assertion. First is his emphasis on the idea of leveling as a vehicle for achieving equality. Leveling is integral to the tribal ethos. That Ibn Khaldun should apply it in the context of a legal proceeding rather than concentrating on one's social status is noteworthy. Lacking actual cases, however, we cannot know how this feature may have been affected by his appraisal of a person's individual character. But while it is uncertain which features of a person's background he might regard as relevant, it is clear that Ibn Khaldun tries to bracket those elements that translate very directly into power differences among contending litigants. Second, he refuses mediation—at least initially—perhaps because here, too, he sees that people may be forced to concede a legitimate legal claim when pressured by the court or a more favorably positioned opponent to reach a settlement. This may also explain why, at least at this stage of a proceeding, he adds his own tactic to the Prophetic injunction counseling settlements by first setting a backdrop of formal adjudication.

If we stand back, then, and consider Ibn Khaldun's approach to law as a test of his more general thinking, several factors commend attention. Ibn Khaldun was nothing if not a proponent of noting connections among seemingly separable domains. In more contemporary terms, he was very much of a functionalist, asking what work things do in society and how they hold a social system together.²⁵ Thus, when, as Bruce Lawrence (2005: ix) notes, he looks at an assessment of events (*khabar*), he asks how they are connected to the customs and traditions of a people, how these in turn build on that consensus to which the Prophet said his community would never agree in error, and how that quest for understanding is constructed out of analogies that keep one firmly rooted in some element of the known. *'Asabiya*, too, comes into play in that the propulsion for solidarity—itself seen as a gift from Allah—is greatly multiplied by religious commitment and hence more likely to complete the Circle of Justice.²⁶ And all of this connects to both inner understanding and adapting to change for a judge who, like the preservers of high Arab literature (*adab*), seeks "to introduce new terms that might reflect the deeper layers of actual experience" (Lawrence 2005: xxiv).

Ibn Khaldun's reliance on assessing persons, which is integral to assessing events, also connects to the style of teaching he commends, for in ordinary education as well as in Sufi instruction, it is through direct contact with a teacher rather than depending on published works that insight may be obtained (Ibn Khaldun 2022: 117ff). As he famously said (Ibn Khaldun 1969: 414): "Among the things that are harmful to the human quest for knowledge and to the attainment of a thorough scholarship are the great number of works available." Similarly, reliance on written maxims of the law—so common among ordinary judges—is seen by Ibn Khaldun as largely insupportable (Shabana 2010: 126–27): Knowledge cannot be separated from the person who possesses it, such that one suspects Ibn Khaldun would not have hesitated to add to the list of qualities both judges and historians should have that which his contemporary Ibn al-Qayyim Jawziyya (d. 1350) called a "knowledge of people" (*ma'rifat al-nās*). In his exercise of a form of holism that anthropologists came to know well, the integration of these disparate features is vital to the world view that suffuses much of Arab culture to this day.

Ibn Khaldun may not be considered an axial figure in the development of such subfields of anthropology as that concerning

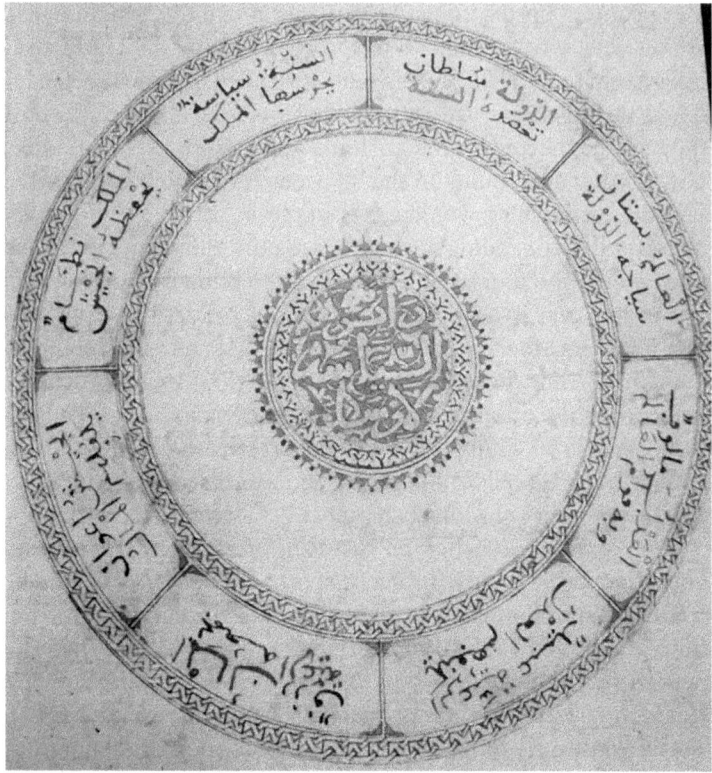

Figure 5.3. The Circle of Justice represents the elements that make possible a peaceful and successful community of believers. Available at https://ballandalus.wordpress.com/2016/07/21/ibn-hajar-al-asqalanis-biography-of-ibn-khaldun-d-8081406/. Public domain.

the relation of law to society, but just as it is unwise to make him into someone who was our contemporary in all matters intellectual so, too, it is an error to ignore the specific ways in which he relates law to society. Many British functionalists ignored history and spoke only of the ethnographic present because if all the features of a society worked to support the existing system it was unclear how one was to account for change as anything but dysfunctional. As Sir Edmund Leach (1954: 282) noted: "We functionalist anthropologists are not really 'antihistorical' by principle; it is simply that we do not know how to fit historical materials into our framework of concepts." Ibn Khaldun, by contrast, could unite functionalism and history, the law being one of the key domains in which he was able to do so. Whereas many later anthropologists have bracketed out law as something with specialized language, specialized personnel, and specialized ways of erasing uncertainty, Ibn Khaldun squarely confronted law as a practical domain that absorbed and reflected many of the contingent—indeed "accidental"—features of the course of history. While his cyclical theory may not appeal to contemporary tastes and his impact on anthropology has remained indirect, there is still much to emulate in his melding of cultural logic with the larger forms that a cultural design may take.

Ibn Khaldun did not solve the problem of how one reconciles the need for a settled legal foundation with the flexibility to do justice to individual cases. But he did believe that if the most corrupting influences at work in a legal system were checked, the Sacred Law and local custom, seen as mutually supportive rather than at loggerheads, were the surest means if not to reverse the course of inevitable dynastic decline at least to retard it. Anthropologists are not in the position of determining the wisdom or the success of such ventures. Through Ibn Khaldun's approach we can, however, see that local practice is part of the law and not an adjunct to it, and through that recognition we can better attend to the full range of factors that inform any legal system and the place it occupies in the larger cultural life of those who have entwined their lives with it.

NOTES

1. Gule (2014: 6), for example, notes that in his *Autobiography* Ibn Khaldun makes no mention of actual legal cases. Malik Ibn Anas (d. 796), the founder of the school of law in which Ibn Khaldun was trained and in which he presided as a judge, had stressed the practice of the Prophet's time and place, but the range was extended over the centuries and collections of actual decisions were prevalent. Ibn Khaldun was thus

trained in a style of law that focused on real cases and not merely abstract jurisprudence. See Fromherz 2010: 49.
2. Elsewhere, Ibn Hajjar described Ibn Khaldun's "love of being contrary in everything." Quoted in Irwin 2019: 105.
3. Amira Bennison (2012) writes: "My own opinion is that Ibn Khaldun comes across as arrogant and devious with a strong tendency to exaggerate his own importance and the flaws of others, but this is as conjectural and subjective as other interpretations of his character which is why [Franz] Rosenthal . . . was wise to warn against elaborating on his personality."
4. Quoted in F. Rosenthal 1984: 16. See Fischel 1967: 34 and Behrens-Abouseif 2023.
5. Morimoto (2002: 115) notes: "Conspiring judges would find the *waqf* contracts of the property in question invalid, or they would give evidence to that effect, so that the property would then be confiscated by the state. History books record cases of such actions being perpetrated even by sultans."
6. Morimoto 2002: 112. In his *Autobiography* (quoted in Morimoto 2002: 121–22) Ibn Khaldun writes:

> Still, I set about . . . arresting the muftis who were quacks or who lacked learning (*ahl al-hawā wa-al-jahl*), and I punished them firmly. Among them, however, was a number of Maghribis [fellow North Africans] who . . . trifled with people's feelings, turning the court (*al-majālis*) into a place where prominent people were slandered and those deserving of respect were insulted. They hated me because of the punishments I meted out, so they joined forces with the inhabitants of those monasteries (*zawāyā*; [more accurately, "religious brotherhoods"]) promoting the same kind of belief as theirs. The appearance of piety that this allegiance lent them brought them a level of prestige, which they then abused in impious ways. Good people (*ahl al-ḥuqūq*) would inevitably choose them as arbitrators, at which they would gabble their chants as if with the voice of Satan, then claim that all was solved. Being unmoved by religion, their ignorance leads them to expose the laws of God (*aḥkām Allāh*) to danger.
>
> I broke up their malevolent circle and chastised their clients, in accordance with the laws of God. Their cronies in the monasteries became powerless, since people stopped going there, so their well [their source of funds] dried up. Having thus lost their clientele these foolish people flew into a rage. They tried to defile my honor, inventing and spreading twisted, false rumors about me. Even the sultan came to hear rumors of my wrongs. The sultan however did not listen to them.

Elsewhere, commentors of his own era wrote: "Ibn Khaldun treated people roughly; he did not rise when the judges came to salute him.... He punished many of the principal clerks and witnesses; he punished the contravention by boxes on the ears and imprisonment. When he was angry against someone he cried, 'Take him to prison,' and was then boxed till his neck was red from pain" (quoted in Enan 1979: 71). On the cases of fraud for which Ibn Khaldun punished officials, see also F. Rosenthal 2000: 47-49.
7. Cited in Fromherz 2010: 100; see also Laabdi 2021: 37–38.
8. Quoted in Fischel 1967: 33.
9. See generally El Hour 2000.
10. Bruce Lawrence's assertion (2005: ix) that "He [Ibn Khaldun] was a juridical activist with a secondary interest in history" is only partially correct. Much depends on which part of his life one is discussing.
11. Talbi 1971: 826, quoting from the *Autobiography*. In his twenties and early thirties, Ibn Khaldun did write several minor treatises, including one on the principles of jurisprudence. See Lakhassi 1996: 353 and Laabdi 2021: 31.
12. On the role of purpose in Islamic legal analysis, see generally Opwis 2010.
13. On the role of contemplation in Islamic legal thought, see Johansen 2013.
14. Except for inheritance and mortmain, Ibn Khaldun seldom discusses specific areas of the law. Torts may be mentioned because one injury might occasion another, thus jeopardizing the peace necessary to *'asabiya* and the avoidance of social chaos, a situation only a strong hand of governance might prevent. We know that as an appellate judge he reviewed sentences from lower court judges, but here too he has rather little to say about criminal law, perhaps, again, because this was a domain where he might have tread too close to the powers of the ruler.
15. As recently as the mid-twentieth century, the famous judge and pasha of Fez, Haj Muhammad al-Baghdadi, was noted for disguising himself, going out into the public, and later surprising dishonest litigants by revealing himself as the man they had also tried to cheat.
16. In another version, the maxim holds that "whatever is dictated by custom (*'urf*) is as if dictated by law." This proposition has been incorporated in a number of Islamic nations' law codes (e.g., the Turkish Majalla 45, Part II). See Gerber 1999: 105 and Shabana 2010: 40.
17. Hourani 1991: 162, quoting Layish and Shmueli 1979.
18. Shabana 2010: 57. For numerous examples of legal scholars relying on custom in specific cases, see Shabana 2010: 55, 98, 120, 123, 153, 156, 159, 162, and 164.

19. Sunan Ibn Majah, chapter 26, hadith no. 2719.
20. Among the sayings attributed to the Prophet about the potential end of Islam are: "The Quran will vanish in one night. No verse in the scripture or in the heart of anyone will be left behind" (Sunan al-Dārimī 3343); "Islam will wear out as embroidery on a garment wears out, until no one will know what fasting, prayer, (pilgrimage) rites and charity are. The Book of Allah will be taken away at night, and not one Verse of it will be left on earth" (Sahih Ibn Majah 3289); "It is narrated on the authority of Ibn 'Umar ('Abdullah b. 'Umar) that the Messenger of Allah observed: Verily Islam started as something strange and it would again revert (to its old position) of being strange just as it started, and it would recede between the two mosques just as thße serpent crawls back into its hole" (Shahih Muslim 1:271).
21. There is one other possible reason why Ibn Khaldun, and indeed the Prophet and Muslims generally, have been so concerned about inheritance. Perhaps, like the Founding Fathers of the United States, they were worried about inherited wealth leading to a highly stratified society, one that would ultimately undermine the unity of the faithful. Indeed, as we will see in a later chapter, it is characteristic of tribal societies or those that maintain a certain tribal ethos to force the levelling of wealth at death both as a means of decentralizing power and to underscore that each individual must build a network of allies and a reputation of reliability for himself, something the consolidation of wealth across generations could undermine to the detriment of society as a whole.
22. "The reliance of sedentary people on laws destroys their fortitude and power of resistance" (Ibn Khaldun 1969: 96).
23. Ibn Khaldun 1958: 2:107; Dale 2015: 250–51. The slide downhill would be catastrophic: "It should be known that this is what the Lawgiver (Muhammad) actually had in mind when he forbade injustice. He meant the resulting destruction and ruin of civilization, which ultimately permits the eradication of the human species" (Ibn Khaldun 1958: 2:107).
24. Quoted in Morimoto 2002: 112.
25. The Arabic term for "function" actually appears repeatedly in his analyses.
26. Although Ibn Khaldun does not employ the circle of justice directly, the concept, which is normally associated with the Ottoman period but actually dates from at least the tenth century CE, resonates with Ibn Khaldun's stress on the interconnectedness of elements in a sociopolitical system and is thus not inconsistent with the tenor of his more explicit propositions. The first full expression of the "circle of justice"

reads as follows (Darling 2012: 3; final line translated by Roger Allen in Himmich 2004: 14):

> The world is a garden, hedged in by sovereignty,
> Sovereignty is lordship, preserved by law,
> Law is administration, governed by the king,
> The king is a shepherd, supported by the army,
> The army are soldiers, fed by money,
> Money is revenue, gathered by the people,
> The people are servants, subjected by justice,
> Justice is happiness, the well-being of the world.
> The world is a garden, with the regime as its fence.

CHAPTER 6

IBN KHALDUN AS AN ARAB THINKER

● ● ●

No theory, no history
—Werner Sombart (1929)

When trying to penetrate the mind of a man who lived over six hundred years ago—especially one who lived in a culture quite unlike one's own—the risk of being anachronistic is ever-present. In Ibn Khaldun's case, with rather little information available about his personality and motivation, we may fill in the blanks too readily. But while keeping in mind both respectful caution and his invitation to use insight to grasp the uncertain, this chapter will seek to understand Ibn Khaldun as a member of his own culture and how, at the same time, he parted company from his contemporaries to achieve his distinctive ideas.

There are three domains that help in seeing Ibn Khaldun's placement within his culture, namely his consideration of time, human psychology, and the nature of relationships. In each of these domains, it will be suggested, he is very much a representative of Arab culture, a culture that has certainly not remained stagnant over the centuries and is certainly variable across the vast expanse from North Africa to the Levant and the Arabian Peninsula. But there are clearly resonances between the Arab cultural assumptions of his day and those of other regions and moments, and if we are careful in our interpolations we may use these features as a test for some of Ibn Khaldun's own orientations and their acceptance or rejection by succeeding generations. Given his role as a historian we may begin most appropriately by looking at the cultural concept of time.

In a striking sentence Ibn Khaldun (1969: 12) says: "The past resembles the future more than one drop of water another." Viewed from the usual perspective, Ibn Khaldun's is a rather simple vision of time as cyclical, where the past and future replicate one another with the regularity of life's usual course. Yes, accidents may derail the straightforward order of repetition, but—at least as it concerns the trajectory of dynasties—only to shift matters onto a parallel path where the cycle can begin all over again. However, it can be argued that this was not the common vision of time in his own era and the way in which he broke with that more accepted view was part of the reason why his concept of history is both distinctive to his work and was not easily acceptable to his contemporaries. Comparisons to non-Muslim and more recent interpretations of Arab ideas of time may help to clarify this point.

In the West, owing in no small part to the development of Christianity, time is largely conceived as directional ("time flies like an arrow") and forward movement is usually equated with morality ("stay on the straight and narrow"). Throughout most of the Middle Ages people "relied on a sense of temporality, an understanding of time, that did not meaningfully distinguish between past, present, and future. But in the late medieval and early modern eras, societies slowly began to shed these characteristics, opening up space for new manners of thought and new forms of belonging" (Huneke 2024). In other parts of the world time is seen as a series of stacked circles, such that (as in the case of the Balinese) where one stands on any given cycle places one closer to others who occupy that same place in the cycle, whether in the future or years gone by, than to contemporaries who are even a small distance away on the same cycle. In each instance, other features of the culture are connected with the view of time. For those whose culture stresses time as directional, positions of political or spiritual power may depend on how far advanced one is in life, while for cultures like the Balinese, the allocation of names, ritual obligations, and forms of symbolic power may be assigned according to one's position in the nested cycles. In the case of the Arabs, by comparison, time is commonly seen as a series of instances in which one is connected to others in an array of constantly negotiated associations that are only as viable as the effectiveness of whoever stands at their center. For many traditional Arab thinkers, in the phrasing of Louis Massignon (1952: 141), "time is not a continuous 'duration,' but a constellation, a 'Milky Way' of instants." History in this view, says Louis Gardet (1976: 212) is largely seen as a "discontinuous succession of experiential 'moments.'"[1] Other cultural features are connected to this rather stochastic view of time. In the Arab case, time is not thought to reveal the truth of persons (hence biography as chronology is less telling than knowing someone's network of obligations), temporal unfolding is not conceived through directional images and metaphors, and inherited position requires separate proof that the attempted transfer of necessary qualities actually took effect.

Within this culture of time, Ibn Khaldun is both a representative adherent and a disturber. He does not favor chronological biography any more than his compatriots as a way of describing history but neither does he settle for plucking out a set of supposedly revealing instances from a life to define the history of that era. He thus appears to share a micro vision of time with the members of his culture that does not rely on time as a scroll that unwinds but challenges their macro view of time by positing a life cycle of regimes no less than of individuals. One may, therefore, speculate that part of the reason Ibn Khaldun's concept of history found rather little impact on the way history was seen by those of the Arab world who shared his lifetime or the many years beyond was that his altered view of time did not fit with theirs, that his rather depersonalized image of time was not how they saw the social world, and that they could not attach other elements of their culture to his vision as easily as could the Western scholars of a much later time.

Change for Ibn Khaldun, as we have seen, is thus not directional. It is true that there are those who have suggested that his comments suggest a form of evolutionism, but the passages they cite are more properly seen as a version of the Great Chain of Being and his general emphasis on social hierarchy.[2] When major change does occur, he consistently argues, it is mainly through accidental occurrence, not something inherent in nature or the course that time must take. Indeed, there is a certain timelessness to the Arab concepts of time upon which he appears to draw. Or, perhaps more accurately, it should be said that time as directional is displaced by relationships, so that the saying among Arabs that "men resemble their times more than they do their fathers" is one that certainly would be compatible with Ibn Khaldun's overall schema. Recall in this regard that he said: "When there is a general change of conditions, it is as if the entire creation had changed and the whole world been altered, as if it were a new and repeated creation, a world brought into existence anew" (Ibn Khaldun 1969: 30). And when change does occur it is a world-changer, not in the sense of altering the generative factors of power but its momentary embodiment.

So, too, Ibn Khaldun expresses a vision of human psychology that has long characterized Islamic thought while also putting his own imprint on the concept. References to human psychology are peppered—directly and indirectly—throughout the *Muqaddima* and his other works (see Nassar 1964). He speaks of how defeat leads to the loss of hope and so deep a feeling of humiliation that one loses all motivation for improving one's situation. He says that "when a nation becomes a victim of psychological defeat, then that marks the end of the nation." The strict enforcement of laws against someone who is defenseless also "generates in that person a feeling of humiliation that, no doubt, must break his fortitude" (Ibn Khaldun 1969: 96). He says that without religious attachment jealousy and envy dominate, but that if taxation is properly calibrated, people "will be psychologically disposed to undertake cultural enterprises because they can be confident of making a profit from them" (1969: 231). His broader theme is particularly evident when he says that good practices become habits and "habits are qualities of the soul" (1969: 318) It is this idea of the "soul" and its conceptual connectors that is worth considering in more detail.

The Arabic term that Ibn Khaldun uses for "soul" is *nafs*, a term and concept that refers to desire and self-respect, life force, breath, and disposition. To have *nafs* is to have self-esteem, but to be in love with one's *nafs* is to be an egoist; to be lacking in *nafs* is to be indecisive, slipshod, cowardly, or impotent. *Nafs* is that vitalizing force that, like any passion or proclivity, can be turned to ends that are good or ill, a quality of flexibility that tracks the notion prevalent in so many Arabic concepts of something whose ambiguity is resolved by the contexts of its use. In modern Arabic the study of *nafs* (*'ilm n-nafs*) is the term used for psychology. Indissolubly linked to *nafs* is the capacity for reason (*'aqel*), itself developed through interaction with wise teachers and mature associates. Suitably nurtured, *'aqel* can channel one's *nafs* into proper choices and is thus vital to the expression of free will. The more common term for "soul" in contemporary North Africa is *ruḥ*, which many people describe as that part of oneself that lives on after death. But Ibn Khaldun's choice of *nafs* for soul is intriguing, not only because he appears to contrast it to the less readily alterable "body" (*jasad*, *badan*) but because it fits with his idea that practice becomes habit which becomes one's settled nature, a concept that conforms to the idea of *nafs* as personhood more than one's immortal soul.[3]

Ibn Khaldun's notion of the self is, then, firmly implanted in the larger set of cultural concepts from which his thinking was derived. Consider, for a moment longer, his emphasis on the role of humiliation in the decline of social solidarity. In an article on the subject, Vivian Gornick (2021: 60) writes:

> Anton Chekhov once observed that the worst thing life can do to human beings is to inflict humiliation. Nothing, nothing, nothing in the world can destroy the soul as much as outright humiliation. Every other infliction can eventually be withstood or overcome, but not humiliation. Humiliation lingers in the mind, the heart, the veins, the arteries forever. It allows people to brood for decades on end, often deforming their inner lives . . . .There are many things we can live without. Self-respect is not one of them.

If one of the meanings Ibn Khaldun attributed to *nafs* was that in its absence one loses self-respect then his usage might accord with the analysis of humiliation rendered by many contemporary analytic psychiatrists. But Ibn Khaldun is more of a social psychologist whose focus remains on the effect humiliation has not just for the individual but for the cohesion that is indispensable to *'asabiya*. Where Gornick cites numerous studies that claim "a national sense of humiliation is, more often than not, a key motive in a country's decision to go to war," Ibn Khaldun—who does not directly address this possibility—sees humiliation instead as the source of societal dissolution.

Indeed, Ibn Khaldun's vision of the individual is not always explicit, quite possibly because he takes as given many of his culture's assumptions about the nature of individuality. For example, I have elsewhere suggested that in contemporary North Africa people think of the self as something that cannot be broken down into completely separable parts (Rosen 1984). To say that a judge might rule in a way that is totally at odds with his personal beliefs or that any individual could segregate his different roles into hermetically sealed domains is not consistent with the view that the self cannot be fractionated in this way. If one reads Ibn Khaldun as accepting as given the idea of the unfractionated self we might understand why he generalizes about human motivation and psychology even though he otherwise acknowledges the intense individuality of the actors he describes. It is not that the individual is swallowed up in the overarching power of *'asabiya* but that individuals reveal themselves in their consolidated personae, that people who are not insane or incompetent do not engage in actions without having the requisite intent necessary for that act, and that one can (as in his Sufi claim that the inner is less subject to choice than the outer) indeed discern another's inner state from a person's overt acts. A closer reading of his work, then, might suggest that his is not simply a universal vision of human motivation and dynastic trajectories but an acute appreciation of how his culture handles the question of the relation of the individual to society as a whole.

In addition to his concepts of time and human psychology, there is a third domain in which we can see how Ibn Khaldun handles the relation of his own culture to the general features of history, namely how relationships are constructed. There is a slight disconnect in the way Ibn Khaldun generalizes about *asabiya* and the way he relates the details of the rise and fall of specific dynasties. In the former, the focus is on broad patterns; in the latter, it is on named individuals and specific histories. Whereas in his general schema *asabiya* requires a leader who consolidates a feeling of solidarity that seems to arise somewhat automatically, in his detailed histories—and certainly in his own relationships—individual maneuvering to advantage is apparent if not emphasized. Indeed, by recognizing a range of ways in which actual regimes and their leaders have maneuvered, Ibn Khaldun may have been expressing less a rigid pattern of dynastic fate than a recognition that for the Arab historian, as for the Arab Everyman, a high degree of toleration for ambiguity may not be out of keeping with an appreciation of individuals and their acts.[4] Once again, his cultural assumption—one that does not require overt articulation—would seem to entail intense individual action. Thus, reading between the lines, we can see how typical his underlying concepts may reflect the assumptions of his culture and the unique way in which he applies them.

If it is accurate to say that Ibn Khaldun sees leaders in particular as needing to go beyond personal network-building to tap into the underlying social and psychological elements of solidarity then we can also see that he has taken the very idea of coalition-building in a unique direction. For he has sought to understand the tools available to the leader in such circumstances and not to rely on that leader's capabilities alone. By merging both the qualities of one who knows the possibilities of *asabiya* when he sees them and the inherent regularities that may render them successful, Ibn Khaldun breaks with the idea of great men making history and forces us to consider what is available in a given culture for such actors to work with. Having served as an envoy to numerous Berber groups and enemies over the course of his career, Ibn Khaldun was only too aware of the idiosyncratic aspects of any relationship but that a shared set of orientations nevertheless makes alliance construction possible. That orientation clearly led him to a very different way of writing history than was true in his own time and one that still has profound lessons for our own forms of social analysis.

Each of these issues remains of vital importance to contemporary anthropology. As we have moved through a variety of disciplinary theories two features have been prevalent. First, that for the most part each has claimed total explanatory power. Whether it is structuralism or cultural evolution, functionalism or biological determinism the lines each has set have rarely been crossed, and the idea of a unified theory of social life, at least since the days of the Social Relations experiment at Harvard, has neither been achieved nor attempted. Ibn Khaldun does not solve this issue, but he does trespass over our later, artificial boundaries without hesitation. He is a functionalist in that he is always asking how a feature contributes to the working of the whole; he is an interpretive scholar when he encourages speculation tempered by his rigorous adherence to the facts as he has come to know them. He is a fieldworker in that he insists upon firsthand contact with the sources of his information, and he is careful to segregate his speculation when he uses the Arabic term *rabbama*, usually translated as "perhaps," to signal a degree of uncertainty. It is inherent in his view of rationality that such boundary crossing is necessary if historical analysis is to break out of the confines within which he envisioned it in his own day.

The second feature concerns the intellectual life course of theories more generally. Stephen Jay Gould once noted that theories are often not proven or disproven but simply set aside as their capacity to produce new information or insights seems to wane. Such theories may, however, be resuscitated, whether because a new generation sees something that resonates with their concerns or because some new data has sparked a review of earlier modes of interpretation. This may be a characteristic of science in some countries or moments more than others. Americans, it has been said, do not so much solve many issues as abandon them. But the kind of issues that Ibn Khaldun raises, however much their attractiveness may wax and wane with the passing of scholarly generations, have a way of coming back to insist on being attended to. So, we may for a time look for grand patterns only to abandon them in favor of minute detail, and then return to formulate some comprehensive scheme. We may disagree as to what is evidence or proof or even worthy of note and follow a research path that takes us into a whole new field only to wonder what comparison dictates that we reconsider. Similarly, Ibn Khaldun embraces a style of analysis and an unrelenting attachment to ferreting out the facts as best he understands them, a style that continues to provide a model of holism anthropologists have at times unwisely forsaken.

Ibn Khaldun, as we have seen, proceeds by fearlessly combining rigorous factual investigation with speculation, in what might otherwise be denominated as the exercise of discretion. In her study of the subject, Lorraine Daston (2023) notes, "When universal rule and particular situation don't align, it's discretion that leaps into the breach. We couldn't live without it. . . . [A]s long as universals can be ambushed by unforeseen particulars, discretion will have to come to the rescue. The only question is whether it does so furtively and secretly or openly, once again recognized and respected as a form of public reason." For Ibn Khaldun the discretion that any historian must exercise is both a responsibility and an opportunity—a responsibility for not misleading the faithful, an opportunity to see both the obvious and the mysterious. He might well have agreed with Ralph Waldo Emerson who said that "In analyzing history, do not be too profound, for often the causes are superficial." But he would also perhaps have accepted Albert Einstein's proposition that "it is the theory which decides what we can observe," and as a result have recognized, as have many social scientists since, that the facts do not simply speak for themselves.

Blending his religiosity with his social analysis also lends a reminder that anthropologists are not infrequently very attached to their religions and that it is from that perspective that some of their greatest insights have developed. One cannot read Mary Douglas on purity and danger, Victor Turner on liminal states, or E. E. Evans-Pritchard on Nuer cosmology without appreciating how their Catholicism led them to analytic concepts that cast light on a wide range of comparative studies; one cannot read Alfonso Ortiz or Akbar Ahmed without seeing how the overtones of their religious attachments molded their choice of topics, evidence, and theory. It is often suggested that Ibn Khaldun was something of an agnostic, and in that respect one is reminded of the Haitian saying, "When the anthropologist arrives, the gods depart." But he was neither an agnostic nor did he bid the gods depart. Rather, he employed his religious orientation to see how the domains of the sacred and the mundane may be practically separable yet ultimately intertwined, and that the insight afforded by the one may yield understanding for the other. It is a lesson that still resonates with many anthropologists.

Finally, one returns to the issue of whether Ibn Khaldun speaks to contemporary concerns or must be seen solely within the context of his own times. The late Egyptian sociologist, Saad Eddin Ibrahim, who started an activist research center in his name, argued that Ibn Khaldun held a key lesson for the present in that a reconstruction of *'asabiya* along updated lines would be indispensable to the progress of his nation (Faruqi 2024). Certainly, some version of *'asabiya* matters to those who have an interest in understanding tribal life, particularly in the Middle East. The *United Nations Arab Human Development Report of 2004*, however, treats *'asabiya* almost exclusively in the outdated sense of clannish behavior and hence as a major impediment to socioeconomic development.

> Clannism, in all its forms, (tribal, clan-based, communal, and ethnic) tightly shackles its followers through the power of the authoritarian patriarchal system . . . . [C]lannism is the enemy of personal independence, intellectual daring, and the flowering of a unique and authentic human entity. It blocks the energies that lead to growth and a mature, self-reliant intellect. It must do this to ensure its own smooth functioning and to guarantee its sway . . . . The problem with clannism in Arab countries is that it produces types of societal organisation that are modern in form but objectively backward. (United Nations 2005: 145–46)

That matters should be put in terms of *'asabiya* underscores the vitality the concept continues to play in contemporary debates among scholars as well as among national and international policy-makers. That the negative aspects of *'asabiya* are now seen, in part, in terms of gender equality and employment opportunities is no less noteworthy than that *'asabiya* should continue to have very positive overtones, even in the UN report, if the beneficial aspects of social cohesion can now include a broader range of players and purposes. Whatever else, it is a tribute to Ibn Khaldun's way of framing the issues that the topics and ideas he developed are still of concern six hundred years after he first enunciated them.

NOTES

1. For additional references and a fuller discussion of some Muslim conceptions of time, see generally Rosen 1984: 172–77.
2. While it is true that Ibn Khaldun said that humans developed from "the world of the monkeys" through a process by which "species become more numerous," Malik (2021: 160–62) is wise to suggest that this is not evolutionism in the Darwinian sense but another example of Ibn Khaldun's hierarchy of substances and creatures akin to the concept of a great chain of being.
3. For more detail on these concepts, see Rosen 1984: 30–47.
4. Ibn Khaldun (1969: 35) says that one of the reasons falsehoods are accepted and transmitted by inept historians "is ignorance of how conditions conform with reality. Conditions are affected by ambiguities and artificial distortions. The informant reports the conditions as he saw them, but on account of artificial distortions he himself has no true picture of them." On the role of ambiguity and ambivalence in Arab culture, see generally Bauer 2021.

CONCLUSION
THE ALLURE OF THE UNIVERSAL, THE TUG OF THE PARTICULAR

● ● ●

The job of the ethnologist is to describe the surface patterns as best he can, to reconstitute the deeper structures out of which they are built, and to classify those structures, once reconstituted, into an analytical scheme.
—Clifford Geertz, *The Interpretation of Cultures*

Tell them the story and happily they will reflect on it.
—*Quran* 7:176

Finding a shorthand way to characterize Ibn Khaldun as a person is not easy; finding a concise way to summarize his ideas has, in many instances, been all too easy. Perhaps, as Robert Irwin (2019: 208) suggests, he was "a strikingly bleak and lonely figure, standing between the exceptional and the conventional, beyond categorisation." Or perhaps the figure dancing on the rooftop and entertaining songsters at his home on the Nile is the real person behind the necessary façade. Perhaps his cyclical theory is circumscribed by a set of inerrant parameters. Or perhaps it is more like the Gulf Stream, that "unbanked river in the sea" whose unpredictable eddies are contained not by clear borders but by friable waves and shifting currents. "Without a profound simplification the world around us would be an infinite undefined tangle that would defy our ability to orient ourselves and decide upon our actions," says Primo Levi: "We are compelled to reduce the knowable to a schema." Ibn Khaldun found in writing both that necessary simplification of a schema and the resultant actions to be taken in its name. He did so in no small part believing that writing is not just a mode of communication but a way of engaging the world of acts: "Writing," he said, "indicates what is in the soul," and even more than the other crafts it "gives intelligence to the person who practices [it]" (Ibn Khaldun 1969: 327 and 331). Indeed, as Allen James Fromherz (2010: 124) notes, "Ibn Khaldun's writing was both intensely contemplative and deliberately public." We might, therefore, regard Ibn Khaldun's years of withdrawal to create the *Muqaddima* less as a retreat than as another form of that worldly engagement he never really left behind.

Ibn Khaldun's mode of expression was also not unconnected to his chosen sources. It is said that one cannot choose one's relatives but one can choose one's ancestors. That privilege is particularly true of authors, for, as Jorge Luis Borges put it, "every writer creates his own precursors." Ibn Khaldun chose his—those teachers whose ideas he accepted, those scholars from the other side of the Mediterranean whose philosophies he admired—and in the process he let his need for clarity and order rather than the constraints of his culture govern his choice of influence. His originality—and his continuing interest to social scientists—lies in no small part in that openness to connective ideas and the effort to employ them in understanding one's own surroundings. Moreover, like many of the anthropologists who followed, Ibn Khaldun was often pulled between the allure of the universal and the tug of the particular. His middle course led him to find a way of attending simultaneously to both, implicitly agreeing with Plato that "if particulars are to have meaning, there must be universals" and that, as a contemporary writer has said, "universals exist according to degrees and particulars exist according to conditions."

Ibn Khaldun sought in Aristotle's emphasis on connections and the middle way a method and a map for making sense of the chaos that engulfed him at every turn. He melded that sensibility with a recognition, common to his culture, that balance is best retained not by stasis but through some form of movement.

Though he does not cite it, he may well have taken to heart that seminal passage in the Quran (2:137) that says: "Thus we appoint you a midmost nation, that you might be a witness to the people, and thus the Messenger might be a witness to you." On its face it sounds as though positioned at the middle must be the easiest of paths: Avoiding extremes one can avoid difficult choices; dodging pitfalls to either side one can easily prevaricate; eschewing attachments on either side, one can claim as the high ground an imagined neutrality. In fact, the very opposite is closer to the truth. For the middle path, whether stretching forth for believer or for scholar, is in fact the most difficult of passages: It demands decisiveness at every step, the capacity to knit together the seemingly irreconcilable without sacrificing principle, the ability to find a basis for uniting groups who must still retain their flexibility through constant re-creation. Whatever its regularities, whatever its destination, Ibn Khaldun's midmost way is not just a path of history but a quest for virtue and reward.

Moreover, Ibn Khaldun was skeptical of all who possessed unwarranted certainty. He chastised those mystics and scholars for seeking certainty in areas where it cannot be found. Whereas admixture is commonly regarded in Islam as one of the dangers to which the pure faith is subject, for Ibn Khaldun realism demands a recognition that an element of the undesirable does not negate the benefits with which it may be entangled (Mufti 2009: 392–93). Just as baser instincts may be needed for proper procreation and acquisitiveness for the fulfillment of needs and obligations to others, so, too, aspects of the political and military that may seem unworthy may still not poison the good they can accomplish. In this, as in his overall recognition of the ambivalent nature of the topics he chose to comprehend, Ibn Khaldun—ever the realist— challenged the simplistic formulas to which generations of scholars continue to be vulnerable.

Human groups will continue to cohere and dissolve, reconstitute themselves and self-destruct. The mysteries they entail have been explored and explanations have been offered over the course of the centuries, and the steps taken to unravel those mysteries will continue to engage the attention of anthropologists and others for many years to come. W. H. Auden wrote: "History is, strictly speaking, the study of questions; the study of answers belongs to anthropology and sociology." Whether one sees him as a successful historian or prescient economist, an early anthropologist or the progenitor of modern sociology, Ibn Khaldun undoubtedly raised the questions and opened doors to invite new answers. He was not always modest about his own achievements. But he also knew his limits and may well have found fellow-feeling in Dorothy Parker's quip that "it is the congenital curse of the writer that whatever he writes is the best that he can do." As for the rest, he said, "only God knows all."

SELECTED WORKS
BY IBN KHALDUN

● ● ●

The following are works by Ibn Khaldun translated into English and French. References to Arabic language editions can be found at Mahdi (1964: 298–99), Fromherz (2010: 181–82), and through related entries in the *Encyclopedia of Islam*. For a discussion of the various translations of Ibn Khaldun's work and an analysis of mainly Arabic-language works of commentary on them see, Abdesselem (1983). Works in the following list will be cited in the present text as Ibn Khaldun followed by the date of one of the references below.

Khaldun, Ibn. 1858. *Prolégomènes d'Ebn Khaldoun*. É. M. Quatremère, ed. Paris: Benjamin Duprat.

———. 1925–1934 [1852–1856]. *Histoire des berbères et des dynasties musulmanes de l'Afrique Septentrionale* [History of the Berbers and Muslim dynasties of North Africa], trans. William McGuckin, le baron de Slane. Paris: Librairie Orientalize Paul Geuthner.

———. 1950. *An Arab Philosophy of History: Selections from the Prolegomena of Ibn Khaldun of Tunis (1332–1406)*, trans. and arr. Charles Issawi. London: John Murray.

———. 1952. *Ibn Khaldun and Tamerlane, Their Historic Meeting in Damascus, 1401 A.D. (803 A.H.): A Study Based on Arabic Manuscripts of Ibn Khaldun's "Autobiography," with a Translation into English, and a Commentary*, trans. Walter J. Fischel. Berkeley: University of California Press.

———. 1958. *The Muqaddimah: An Introduction to History*, 3 vols., trans. Franz Rosenthal. New York: Pantheon.

———. 1969. *The Muqaddimah: An Introduction to History*, trans. Franz Rosenthal, ed. and abr. N. J. Dawood. Princeton, NJ: Princeton University Press.

———. 1975. *Discours sur l'histoire universelle: Al-Muqaddima*, new translation, préface and notes by Vincent Monteil. Paris: Sindbad.

———. 1980. *Le voyage d'Occident et d'Orient*, trans. Abdesselam Cheddadi of the *Autobiography* [*al-Ta'rif bi Ibn Khaldun*]. Paris: Sindbad.

———. 1986. *Peuples et nations du monde: extraits des Kitāb al-'Ibar*, vols. 1 and 2. Selected, presented, translated from Arabic and annotated by Abdesselam Cheddadi. Paris: Sindbad.

———. 1990. Adal, Youmna A. "Sufism in Ibn Khaldun: An Annotated Translation of the "Shifa' al-Sa'il li-Tahdhib al-Masa'il." Ph.D. dissertation. Bloomington: Indiana University. Retrieved 7 March 2025 from https://www.proquest.com/openview/179e6c27d26eb51df2f449bab0e7b671/1?pqorigsite=gscholar&cbl=18750&diss=y. Retrieved 7 March 2025 from https://archive.org/stream/SUFISMINIBNKHALDUN_201710/SUFISM%20IN%20IBN%20KHALDUN_djvu.txt.

———. 1991. *La voie et la loi, ou, Le maître et le juriste* [*Shifâ' al-sâ'il li-tahdhîb al-masâ'il*; The way and the law, or, The master and the jurist], trans. and ann. René Pérez. Paris: Sindbad.

———. 2002. *Le livre des exemples* [*Kitāb al-'Ibar*; The book of examples], trans. and ann. Abdesselem Cheddadi. Paris: Gallimard.

———. 2005. *Al-Muqaddimah*, 3 vols, ed. Abdesselam Cheddadi. Casablanca: Bayt Al-Funûn wa'l-Ulûm wa'l-Adab.

———. 2006. *Autobiographie*, pres., trans., and ann. Abdesselem Cheddadi. Temara, Morocco: Maison des Arts, des Sciences et des Lettres.

———. 2014. "The Scholar and the Sultan: A Translation of the Historic Encounter between Ibn Khaldun and Timur." [Mohamad Ballan's revision of Fischel's 1952 translation of an extract from the *Autobiography*.] *Ballandalus*, 30 August. Retrieved 7 March 2025 from https://ballandalus.wordpress.com/2014/08/30/the-scholar-and-the-sultan-a-translation-of-the-historic-encounter-between-ibn-khaldun-and-timur/.

———. 2017. *Ibn Khaldūn on Sufism: Remedy for the Questioner in Search of Answers* (*Shifā' al-saʾil li- tahdhīb al-masā'il*), trans. Yumna Özer. Cambridge: The Islamic Texts Society.

———. 2022. *The Requirements of the Sufi Path: A Defense of the Mystical Tradition*, ed. and trans. Carolyn Baugh. New York: New York University Press.

REFERENCES

Almost all of the items noted here are cited somewhere in this book. Others, however, are included as a guide to further reading, their titles being indicative of the topics they entertain.

Abdesselem, Ahmed. 1983. *Ibn Khaldun et ses lectures*. Paris: Presses Universitaires de France.
Aberle, David F., A.K. Cohen, A.K. Davis, M.J. Levy, Jr ., and F.X. Sutton. 1950. "The Functional Prerequisites of a Society." *Ethics* 60(2): 100–11.
Abou-Tabickh, Lilian. 2019. "*Al-'Aṣabiyya* in Context: Choice and Historical Continuity in *Al-Muqaddima* of Ibn Khaldūn." Ph.D. dissertation. Toronto: University of Toronto. Retrieved 7 March 2025 from https://tspace.library.utoronto.ca/bitstream/1807/97302/1/Abou-Tabickh_Lilian_%20_201911_PhD_thesis.pdf.
Ahearn, Laura. 2010. "Agency and Anthropology." *Annual Review of Anthropology* 30: 109–37.
Ahmad, Zaid. 2004. *The Epistemology of Ibn Khaldun*. London: Routledge.
———. 2017. "A 14th Century Critique of Greek Philosophy: The Case of Ibn Khaldun." *Journal of Historical Sociology* 30(1): 57–66.
Ahmed, Akbar S. 2002. "Ibn Khaldun's Understanding of Civilizations and the Dilemmas of Islam and the West Today." *Middle East Journal* 56(1): 20–45.
———. 2005. "Ibn Khaldun and Anthropology: The Failure of Methodology in the Post 9/11 World." *Contemporary Sociology* 34(6): 591–96.
Alam, Manzoor. 1997. "Ibn Khaldun on the Origin, Growth and Decay of Cities." In *Encyclopedic Survey of Islamic Culture, Vol. 5: Medieval Muslim Historiography*, ed. Mohamed Taher, 229–47. New Delhi: Anmol Publications Pvt. Limited.

Alatas, Syed Farid. 2001. "Introduction to the Political Economy of Ibn Khaldun." *Islamic Quarterly* 45(4): 307–24.

———. 2013. *Ibn Khaldun*. New Delhi: Oxford University Press.

———. 2014. *Applying Ibn Khaldun: The Recovery of a Lost Tradition in Sociology*. London: Routledge.

Al-Azmeh, Aziz. 1981. *Ibn Khaldun in Modern Scholarship: A Study in Orientalism*. London: Third World Centre for Research and Pub.

———. 1990. *Ibn Khaldūn: An Essay in Reinterpretation*. London: Routledge.

———. 1993. *Ibn Khaldūn*. Cairo: American University in Cairo Press.

Amri, Laroussi. 2008. "The Concept of 'Umran: The Heuristic Knot in Ibn Khaldun." *The Journal of North African Studies* 13(3): 345–55.

Anderson, Jon. 1984. "Conjuring with Ibn Khaldun: From an Anthropological Point of View." In *Ibn Khaldun and Islamic Ideology*, ed. Bruce Lawrence, 111–21. Leiden: Brill.

Asatrian, Mushegh. 2003. "Ibn Khaldun on Magic and the Occult." *Iran and the Caucasus* 7(1–2): 73–123.

Ayalon, David. 1980a. "Mamlukiyyat (B) Ibn Khaldun's View of the Mamluk Phenomenon." *Jerusalem Studies in Arabic and Islam* 2: 340–49.

———. 1980b. "The Mamluks and Ibn Xaldun." *Israel Oriental Studies* 10: 11–13.

Baali, Fuad, and Ali Wardi. 1981. *Ibn Khaldun and Islamic Thought-Styles: A Social Perspective*. Boston: G. K. Hall and Co.

Bae, Bosco B. 2016. "Believing Selves and Cognitive Dissonance: Connecting Individual and Society via 'Belief.'" *Religions* 7(7): 86. https://doi.org/10.3390/rel7070086.

Ballan, Mohamad. 2019. "The Scribe of the Alhambra: Lisān al-Dīn ibn al-Khaṭīb, Sovereignty and History in Nasrid Granada." Unpublished Ph.D. dissertation. Chicago: University of Chicago. https://doi.org/10.6082/uchicago.1702.

———. 2023. "Borderland Anxieties: Lisān al-Dīn ibn al-Khaṭīb (d. 1374) and the Politics of Genealogy in Late Medieval Granada." *Speculum* 98(2): 447–95.

Ballandalus. 2016. "Ibn Hajar al-Asqalani's Biography of Ibn Khaldun (d. 808/1406)." *Ballandalus*, 21 July. Retrieved 7 March 2025 from https://ballandalus.wordpress.com/2016/07/21/ibn-hajar-al-asqalanis-biography-of-ibn-khaldun-d-8081406/.

Bartra, Roger. 2014. *Anthropology of the Brain*. Cambridge: Cambridge University Press.

Bauer, Thomas. 2021. *A Culture of Ambiguity: An Alternative History of Islam*. New York: Columbia University Press.

Behrens-Abouseif, Doris. 2019. "Review of Robert Irwin, *Ibn Khaldun: An Intellectual Biography*." *Journal of the Royal Asiatic Society* 29(1): 187–88.

———. 2023. *Dress and Dress Code in Medieval Cairo: A Mamluk Obsession*. Leiden: Brill.

Bennison, Amira K. 2012. "Review of Allen James Fromherz, *Ibn Khaldun, Life and Times*." *Journal of Islamic Studies* 23(1): 98–100.

———. 2016. *The Almoravid and Almohad Empires*. Edinburgh: Edinburgh University Press.

Ben Salem, Lilia. 1973. "La notion de pouvoir dans l'oeuvre d'Ibn Khaldūn" [The notion of power in the work of Ibn Khaldūn]. *Cahiers Internationaux de Sociologie* 55: 293–314.

Berger, Marcos Guevara. 2021. "Judicial Representations of Culture." In *Culture as Judicial Evidence: Expert Testimony in Latin America*, ed. Leila Rodriguez, 19–54. Cincinnati: University of Cincinnati Press.

Berliner, David, ed. 2016. "Anthropology and the Study of Contradictions." *Hau: Journal of Ethnographic Theory* 6(1): 1–27.

Berque, Jacques. 1947. "Ibn Khaldun et les Bédouins de Maghreb." *Histoire et Société* 48–64.

———. 1974. *Maghreb, histoire et sociétés*. Gembloux: Duculot.

Bidney, David, ed. 1963. *The Concept of Freedom in Anthropology*. The Hague: Mouton.

———. 1995. *Theoretical Anthropology*, 2nd edn. New Brunswick, NJ: Transaction Pub.

Boas, Franz. 1945. *Race and Democratic Society*. New York: J. J. Augustin.

Bonte, Pierre. 2003. "Ibn Khaldun and Contemporary Anthropology: Cycles and Factional Alliances of Tribe and State in the Maghreb." In *Tribes and Power: Nationalism and Ethnicity in the Middle East*, ed. Faleh Abdul-Jabar and Hosham Dawod, 50–66. London: Saqi.

Boulakia, Jean David C. 1971. "Ibn Khaldūn: A Fourteenth Century Economist." *The Journal of Political Economy* 79(5): 1105–18.

Bouthoul, Gaston. 1930. *Ibn Khaldoun: sa philosophie sociale*. Paris: Geuthner.

Bozarslan, Hamit. 2014. *Le luxe et le violence: domination et contestation chez Ibn Khaldun* [Luxury and violence: Domination and contestation in Ibn Khaldun]. Paris: CNRS.

Brett, Michael. 1995. "The Way of the Nomad." *Bulletin of the School of Oriental and African Studies* 58(2): 251–69.

———. 1999. *Ibn Khaldun and the Medieval Maghrib*. Aldershot, UK: Ashgate/Variorum.

Brunschvig, Robert. 1940–47. *La Berbérie orientale sous les Ḥafṣides des origines à la fin du XV siècle* [Eastern North Africa under the Ḥafṣids from the origins to the end of the 15th century], 2 vols. Paris: Adrien-Maisonneuve.

Çaksu, Ali. 2017. "Ibn Khaldun and Philosophy: Causality in History." *Journal of Historical Sociology* 30(1): 27–42.

Campbell, Joseph Keim, Michael O'Rourke, David Shier, et al., eds. 2004. *Freedom and Determinism*. Cambridge, MA: The MIT Press.

Capezzione, Leonardo. 2020. "The City and the Law: Aspects of Ibn Khaldūn's Critique of the Philosophers." *Philological Encounters* 5: 4–24.

Chaouch, Khalid. 2008. "Ibn Khaldun, In Spite of Himself." *Journal of North African Studies* 13(3): 279–91.

Cheddadi, Abdesselam. 1980. "Le système de pouvoir en Islam d'apres Ibn Khaldûn" [The system of power in Islam according to Ibn Khaldun]. *Annales, Economies, Société, Civilisations* 35: 534–50.

———. 1999. *Ibn Khaldûn revisité*. Casablanca: Les Editions Toubkal.

———. 2005. "Reconnaissance d'Ibn Khaldûn." *Esprit* 11: 1–11. Translated into English as "Recognizing the Importance of Ibn Khaldun." Retrieved 7 March 2025 from https://www.diplomatie.gouv.fr/IMG/pdf/Cheddadieng.pdf.

———. 2006a. *Actualite' d'Ibn Khaldûn: conférences et entretiens* [Ibn Khaldûn news: Conferences and interviews]. Alger: C.N.R.P.A.H.

———. 2006b. *Ibn Khaldun: l'homme et le théoricien de la civilization* [Ibn Khaldun: The man and the theorist of civilization]. Paris: Gallimard.

———. 2016. *Ibn Khaldoun: une biographie romancée* [Ibn Khaldoun: A fictionalized biography]. Casablanca: Editions la Croisée des Chemins.

———. 2021. "Ibn Khaldun, 'Abd al-Raḥmān." *Encyclopaedia of Islam Three Online*. https://doi-org.ezproxy.princeton.edu/10.1163/1573-3912_ei3_COM_30943.

———. 2024. *The World until 1400 according to Ibn Khaldun: A Global History of Humanity*. London: Routledge.

Collini, Stefan. 2011. "What's Not to Like? Review of Ernest Gellner: An Intellectual Biography." *London Review of Books* 33(11): June 2.

cooke, miriam. 1984. "Ibn Khaldun and Language: From Linguistic Habit to Philological Craft." In *Ibn Khaldun and Islamic Ideology*, ed. Bruce Lawrence, 27–36. Leiden: Brill.

———. 2014. *Tribal Modern: Branding New Nations in the Arab Gulf*. Berkeley: University of California Press.

Dale, Stephen Frederic. 2006. "Ibn Khaldun: The Last Greek and the First *Annaliste* Historian." *International Journal of Middle East Studies* 38: 431–61.

———. 2015. *The Orange Trees of Marrakech: Ibn Khaldun and the Science of Man*. Cambridge, MA: Harvard University Press.

Darling, Linda. 2012. *A History of Social Justice and Political Power in the Middle East: The Circle of Justice from Mesopotamia to Globalization*. New York: Routledge.

Daston, Lorraine. 2022. *Rules: A Short History of What We Live By*. Princeton, NJ: Princeton University Press.

———. 2023. "The Virtue of Discretion." *Aeon*, 21 April.

de Cillis, Maria. 2017. *Free Will and Predestination in Islamic Thought*. London: Routledge.

Dhaouadi, Mahmoud. 2005. "The *Ibar*: Lessons of Ibn Khaldun's Umran Mind." *Contemporary Sociology* 34(6): 585–91.

Dover, Cedric. 1952. "The Racial Philosophy of Ibn Khaldun." *Phylon* 13(2): 107–19.

El Hour, Rachid. 2000. "The Andalusian Qāḍī in the Almoravid Period: Political and Judicial Authority." *Studia Islamica* 90: 67–83.

El-Rayes, Waseem. 2013. "The *Book of Allusions*: A New Translation of the Title to Ibn Khaldun's *Kitab al-'Ibar*." *Religious Studies and Theology* 32(1): 163–84.

Enan, Mohammad Abdullah. 1979. *Ibn Khaldun: His Life and Work*. New Delhi: Kitab Bhavan.

Enderwitz, Susanne. 2019. "'Abd al-Rahman Ibn Khaldūn (8th/14th Century) [The Autobiography]." In *Handbook of Autobiography, Vol. 3, 1397–1409*, ed. Martina Wagner-Egelhaaf, 1397–1409. Berlin: De Gruyter.

Evans-Pritchard, E. E. 1937. *Witchcraft, Oracles and Magic among the Azande*. Oxford: Clarendon Press.

Faruqi, Daanish. 2024. "The Contradictory Legacy of an Egyptian Sociologist." *New Lines Magazine*, 27 September. Retrieved 7 March 2025 from https://newlinesmag.com/essays/the-contradictory-legacy-of-an-egyptian-sociologist/.

Fierro, Maribel. 2007. "Idra'ū l-ḥudūd bi-l-shubuhāt: When Lawful Violence Meets Doubt." *Hawwa* 5(2–3): 208–38.

Firth, Raymond. (1951) 1963. *Elements of Social Organization*. Boston: Beacon Press.

Fischel, Walter J. 1952. *Ibn Khaldun and Tamerlane, Their Historic Meeting in Damascus, 1401 A.D. (803 A.H.): A Study Based on Arabic Manuscripts of Ibn Khaldun's "Autobiography," with a Translation into English, and a Commentary*. Berkeley: University of California Press.

———. 1956. "Ibn Khaldūn on the Bible, Judaism and the Jews." In *Goldziher Memorial Volume, Part II*, ed. Samuel Lowinger, J. Somogyi, and A. Scheiber, 147–71. Jerusalem: Rubin Mass.

———. 1967. *Ibn Khaldun in Egypt: His Public Functions and His Historical Research (1382–1406), A Study in Islamic Historiography*. Berkeley: University of California Press.

Fleischer, Cornell. 1984. "Royal Authority, Dynastic Cyclism, and 'Ibn Khaldûnism' in Sixteenth-Century Ottoman Letters." In *Ibn Khaldun and Islamic Ideology*, ed. Bruce Lawrence, 46–68. Leiden: E. J. Brill.

Fromherz, Allen James. 2010. *Ibn Khaldun, Life and Times*. Edinburgh: Edinburgh University Press.

Gardet, Louis. 1976. "Moslem Views of Time and History." In *Cultures and Time*, ed. L. Gardet, P. Ricoeur, C. Larre, R. Panikkar, et al. Paris: Unesco Press.

Gates, Warren E. 1967. "The Spread of Ibn Khaldun's Ideas on Climate and Culture." *Journal of the History of Ideas* 28(3): 415–22.

Geertz, Clifford. 1968. "Thinking as a Moral Act: Ethical Dimensions of Anthropological Fieldwork in the New States." *The Antioch Review* 28(2): 139–58.

———. 1984. "Anti Anti-Relativism." *American Anthropologist*, New Series 86(2): 263–78.

Gellner, Ernest. 1961. "From Ibn Khaldūn to Karl Marx." *Political Quarterly* 32: 385–92.

———. 1975. "Cohesion and Identity: The Maghreb from Ibn Khaldun to Emile Durkheim." *Government and Opposition* 10(2): 203–18.

———. 1981. *Muslim Society*. Cambridge: Cambridge University Press.

———. 1988. *Plough, Sword and Book*. London: Collins Harvill.

———. 1996. *Anthropology and Politics: Revolution in the Sacred Grove*. Oxford: Blackwell.

Gerber, Haim. 1999. *Islamic Law and Culture 1600–1840*. Leiden: E. J. Brill.

Ghamdi, Saleh Mued. 1989. *Autobiography in Classical Arabic Literature: An Ignored Literary Genre*. Ann Arbor, MI: UMI.

Ghazoul, Ferial. 1984. "The Metaphors of Historiography: A Study of Ibn Khaldun's Historical Imagination." In *In Quest of an Islamic Humanism*, ed. A. H. Green, 48–61. Cairo: American University of Cairo Press.

Gibb, Hamiliton A. R. (1933) 1962. "The Islamic Background of Ibn Khaldun's Political Theory." Reprinted from *The Bulletin of the School of Oriental and African Studies* 7(1): 22–31. In *Studies on the Civilization of Islam*. Boston: Beacon Press.

Gierer, Alfred. 2001. "Ibn Khaldūn on Solidarity ('Asabiyah')—Modern Science on Cooperativeness and Empathy: A Comparison." *Philosophia Naturalis* 38: 91–104.

Gimaret, Daniel. 1980. *Théories de l'acte humain en théologie musulmane* [Theories of human action in Muslim theology]. Paris: Librairie Philosophique.
Goitein, S. D. 1977. "Individualism and Conformity in Classical Islam." In *Individualism and Conformity in Classical Islam*, ed. Amin Banani and Spyros Vryonis, 3–17. Wiesbaden: Otto Harrassowitz.
Goodman, Lenn Evan. 1972. "Ibn Khaldūn and Thucydides." *Journal of the American Oriental Society* 92(2): 250–70.
Gornick, Vivian. 2021. "'Put on the Diamonds': Notes on Humiliation." *Harper's Magazine* October: 59–65.
Graeber, David, and Marshall Sahlins. 2017. *On Kings*. Chicago: HAU.
Gule, Lars. 2015. "Ibn Khaldun: Law and Justice in the Science of Civilisation." In *Philosophy of Justice* (Contemporary Philosophy, A New Survey Book 12), ed. Guttorm Fløistad, 119–38. Dordrecht: Springer. Pagination employed in this book follows the online copy. Retrieved 7 March 2025 from https://link.springer.com/book/10.1007/978-94-017-9175-5.
Hamès, Constant. 1987. "La filiation généalogique (*nasab*) dans la société d'Ibn Khaldūn" [Genealogical filiation in Ibn Khaldūn's society]. *L'Homme*, 27e Année, No. 102: 99–118.
Hamli, Mohsen. 2008. "Demystifiying Ibn Khaldun's Version of al-Kahena." *Journal of North African Studies* 13(3): 309–18.
Hannoum, Abdelmajid. 2001. *Colonial Histories, Postcolonial Memories: The Legend of the Kahina, a North African Heroine*. Westport, CT: Greenwood.
———. 2003. "Translation and the Colonial Imaginary: Ibn Khaldun Orientalist." *History and Theory* 42(1): 61–81.
———. 2021. *The Invention of the Maghreb: Between Africa and the Middle East*. Cambridge: Cambridge University Press.
———. 2022. "The *Muqaddima* of Ibn Khaldûn." *Classical Texts in Context. Bloomsbury History: Theory and Method*. London: Bloomsbury Publishing. https://doi.org/10.5040/9781350915831.160.
———. 2023. *Secular Narrations and Transdisciplinary Knowledge*. London: Routledge.
Hardy, Paul. 2002. "Medieval Muslim Philosophers on Race." In *Philosophers on Race: Critical Essays*, ed. Julie K. Ward and Tommy L. Lott, 38–62. Oxford: Blackwell Publishers.
Harris, Sam. 2012. *Free Will*. New York: Free Press.
High, Casey. 2010. "Agency and Anthropology: Selected Bibliography." *Ateliers d'Anthropologie* 34. https://journals.openedition.org/ateliers/8516.

Himmich, Bansalem. 2004. *The Polymath*, trans. Roger Allen. Cairo: The American University in Cairo Press.

Hirschberg, H. Z. 1963. "The Problem of the Judaized Berbers." *The Journal of African History* 4(3): 313–39.

Hobsbawm, Eric. 2011. "Reflections on a Mughal Portrait." In *Reflections on Islamic Art*, ed. Ahdaf Soueif, 85–89. Doha, Qatar: Bloomsbury Qatar Foundation Publishing.

Hocart, A. M. (1952) 1970. *The Life-Giving Myth and Other Essays*. London: Tavistock and Methuen.

Hopkins, Nicholas S. 1990. "Engels and Ibn Khaldun." *Alif: Journal of Comparative Poetics* 10: 9–18.

Horrut, Claude. 2006. *Ibn Khaldūn, un Islam des "Lunières."* Paris: Les Éditions Complexes.

Hourani, Albert. 1991. *A History of the Arab Peoples*. Cambridge, MA: Harvard University Press.

Huneke, Samuel Clowes. 2024. "Reading [Benedict Anderson's] *Imagined Communities* amid a Resurgence of Nationalism." *The New Republic*, 10 April.

Ibrahim, Ahmed Fekry. 2019. "Legal Pluralism in Sunni Islamic Law: The Causes and Functions of Juristic Disagreement." In *Routledge Handbook of Islamic Law*, ed. Khaled Abou El Fadl, Ahmad Atif Ahmad, and Said Fares Hassan. 208–20. London: Routledge.

Ibn Hajar al-Asqalani. 2016. *Ibn Hajar al-Asqalani's Biography of Ibn Khaldun (d. 808/1406)*, trans. Mohamad Ballan. Ballandalus. "Ibn Hajar al-Asqalani's Biography of Ibn Khaldun (d. 808/1406)." *Ballandalus*, 21 July. Retrieved 7 March 2025 from https://ballandalus.wordpress.com/2016/07/21/ibn-hajar-al-asqalanis-biography-of-ibn-khaldun-d-8081406/.

Irwin, Robert. 1997. "Toynbee and Ibn Khaldun." *Middle Eastern Studies* 33(3): 461–79.

———. 2019. *Ibn Khaldun: An Intellectual Biography*. Princeton, NJ: Princeton University Press.

Issawi, Charles, trans. 1950. *An Arab Philosophy of History: Selections from the Prolegomena of Ibn Khaldun of Tunis (1332–1406)*. London: John Murray.

Johansen, Baber. 2013. "Dissent and Uncertainty in the Process of Legal Norm Construction in Muslim Sunni Law." In *Law and Tradition in Classical Islamic Thought*, ed. Michael Cook, N. Haider, I. Rabb, and A. Sayeed. 127–44. New York: Palgrave MacMillan.

Johnson, Adayshia. 2022. "Ibn Khaldun's Views on Race: Influences by Early Life/Childhood, Climate, Geography, and Geographic Segmentation." *The Macksey Journal* 3(1): 1–7.

Johnson, Steve. 1991. "The 'Umranic Nature of Ibn Khaldun's Classification of the Sciences." *The Muslim World* 81: 254–61.
Journal of Historical Sociology. 2017. "Special Issue: Ibn Khaldun: Theory and Methodology." *Journal of Historical Sociology* 30(1): 1–106. https://doi.org/10.1111/johs.12149.
Journal of North African Studies. 2008. "The Worlds of Ibn Khaldun." *The Journal of North African Studies* 13(3): 275–408.
Kahlaoui, Tarek. 2008. "Towards Reconstructing the Muqaddimah Following Ibn Khaldun's Reading of the Idrisian Text and Maps." *The Journal of North African Studies* 13(3): 293–307.
Katsiaficas, George. 2001. "Ibn Khaldun: A Dialectical Philosopher for the New Millenium." In *Explorations in African Political Thought*, ed. Teodros Kiros, 55-68. New York: Routledge.
Khalil, Elias L. 2007. "Ibn Khaldûn on Property Rights: The Muqaddimah, An Introduction to History." *Journal of Institutional Economics* 3(2): 227–38.
Khomeini, Sayyid Ruhullah Musawi. 1939. "Forty Hadith, An Exposition. Second Revised Edition." *Al-Islam.org*. Retrieved 7 March 2025 from https://www.al-islam.org/forty-hadith-exposition-second-revised-edition-sayyid-ruhullah-musawi-khomeini/eighth-hadith.
Kilpatrick, Hilary. 1991. "Autobiography and Classical Arabic Literature." *Journal of Arabic Literature* 22(1): 1–20.
Knysh, Alexander. 2018. *Sufism: A New History of Islamic Mysticism*. Princeton, NJ: Princeton University Press.
Krugman, Paul. 2013. "Ibn Khaldun, Psychohistorian." *New York Times*, 25 August.
Laabdi, Mourad. 2018. *"'lm al-khilāf* / Legal Controversy." In *Oxford Online Bibliographies in Islamic Studies*, ed. John O. Voll. Oxford: Oxford University Press. http://www.oxfordbibliographies.com/view/document/obo-9780195390155/obo-9780195390155-0257.xml.
———. 2021. "Ibn Khaldun between Legal Theory and Legal Practice." *Journal of Islamic Studies* 32(1): 27–61.
Lacoste, Yves. 1984. *Ibn Khaldun: The Birth of History and the Past of the Third World*. London: Verso.
Lahbabi, Mohamed-Aziz. 1987. *Ibn Khaldūn: notre contemporain*. Paris: L'Harmattan.
Lakhsassi, Abderrahmane. 1996. "Ibn Khaldun." In *History of Islamic Philosophy*, vol. 1, ed. Sayyed Hossein Nasr and Oliver Leaman, 350–64. London: Routledge.
Lawrence, Bruce. 1983. "Introduction: Ibn Khaldun and Islamic Ideology." *Journal of Asian and African Studies* 18(3–4): 154–65.
———. ed. 1984. *Ibn Khaldun and Islamic Ideology*. Leiden: E. J. Brill.

———. 2005. "Introduction to the 2005 Edition." In *The Muqaddimah*, abridged edition, ed. Franz Rosenthal, vii–xxv. Princeton, NJ: Princeton University Press.

Layish, Aharon, and A. Shmueli. 1979. "Custom and *Shari'a* in the Bedouin Family according to Legal Documents from the Judaean Desert." *Bulletin of the School of Oriental and African Studies (SOAS)* 42: 29–45.

Leach, Edmund. 1954. *Political Systems of Highland Burma*. Boston: Beacon Press.

Lee, Dorothy D. 1987. *Freedom and Culture*. New York: Waveland.

Leezenberg, Michiel. 2021. Review of Robert Irwin, *Ibn Khaldun: An Intellectual Biography*. *History of Humanities* 6(1): 346–48.

Lelli, Giovanna. 2021. *Knowledge and Beauty in Classical Islam: An Aesthetic Reading of the Muqaddima of Ibn Khaldun*. London: Routledge.

Libson, Gideon. 1997. "On the Development of Custom as a Source of Law in Islamic Law: Al-rujū'u ilā al-'urfi aḥadu al-qawā'idi al-khamsi allatī yatabannā 'alayhā al-fiqhu." *Islamic Law and Society* 4(2): 131–55.

Machouche, Salah, and Benaouda Bensaid. 2015. "The Roots and Constructs of Ibn Khaldūn's Critical Thinking." *Intellectual Discourse* 23(2): 201–28.

Mahdi, Muhsin. (1957) 1964. *Ibn Khaldûn's Philosophy of History*. Chicago: University of Chicago Press.

———. 1968. "Ibn Khaldun." In *International Encyclopedia of the Social Sciences*, ed. David L. Sills and Robert K. Merton, 53–57. New York: The Macmillan Company and The Free Press.

Malešević, Siniša. 2022. "War, Violence and Group Solidarity: From Ibn Khaldun to Ernest Gellner and Beyond." In *Ernest Gellner's Legacy and Social Theory Today*, ed. Petr Skalník, 241–69. New York: Palgrave MacMillan.

Malik, Shoaib Ahmed. 2021. *Islam and Evolution: Al-Ghazālī and the Modern Evolutionary Paradigm*. London: Routledge.

Mallat, Natalie. 2023. "Mamluk-Italian Relations: The Untold Story of the Renaissance." *Biblioteca Natalie*, 13 May. Retrieved 7 March 2025 from https://bibliotecanatalie.com/f/de-medici-da-vinci-and-mamluk-sultan-qaitbay?blogcategory=Arab.

Mamdani, Mahmood. 2017. "Reading Ibn Khaldun in Kampala." *Journal of the History of Sociology* 30: 7–26.

Marmura, Michael E. 1968. "Causation in Islamic Thought." In *Dictionary of the History of Ideas*, vol. 1, ed. Philip P. Weiner, 286–89. New York: Scribners.

Marozzi, Justin. 2004. *Tamerlane: Sword of Islam, Conqueror of the World*. New York: Da Capo Press.

Martinez-Gros, Gabriel. 2012. "L-État et ses tribus, ou le devinir tribal du monde, Reflexions à partir d'Ibn Khaldoun" [The State and its tribes, or the tribal destiny of the world, reflections from Ibn Khaldoun]. *Esprit* 1: 25–42.

Massignon, Louis. 1952. "Le temps dans la pensée Islamique" [Time in Islamic thought] *Eranos-Jahrbuch 1951* 20: 141–48. Zurich: Rhein-Verlag.

McCorriston, Joy. 2013. "Pastoralism and Pilgrimage: Ibn Khaldun's Bayt-State Model and the Rise of the Arabian Kingdoms." *Current Anthropology* 54(5): 607–41.

McKenna, Michael, and D. Justin Coates. 2020. "Compatibilism." In *The Stanford Encyclopedia of Philosophy* (Spring Edition), ed. Edward N. Zalta. Retrieved 7 March 2025 from https://plato.stanford.edu/entries/compatibilism/.

Mele, Alfred R., ed. 2015. *Surrounding Free Will*. Oxford: Oxford University Press.

Messier, Ronald A. 2001. "Re-Thinking the Almoravids, Re-Thinking Ibn Khaldun." In *North Africa, Islam and the Mediterranean World: From the Almoravids to the Algerian War*, ed. Julia Clancy-Smith, 59–79. London: Frank Cass.

Meuleman, Johan H. 1991. "La causalité dans la Muqaddimah d'Ibn Khaldun." *Studia Islamica* 74: 105–42.

Meyerhof, Max, and Joseph Schacht. 1937. *The Medico-Philosophical Controversy between Ibn Butlan of Baghdad and Ibn Ridwan of Cairo: A Contribution to the History of Greek Learning among the Arabs*. Cairo: Egyptian University Faculty of Arts, Publication No. 13.

Mojuetan, B. A. 1981. "Ibn Khaldun and His Cycle of Fatalism: A Critique." *Studia Islamica* 53: 93–108.

Montague, Ashley, ed. 1956. *Toynbee and History: Critical Essays and Reviews*. Boston: Porter Sargent.

Morimoto, Kosei. 2002. "What Ibn Khaldūn Saw: The Judiciary of Mamluk Egypt." *Mamluk Studies Review* 6: 109–31.

Morris, James Winston. 2009. "An Arab Machiavelli? Rhetoric, Philosophy and Politics in Ibn Khaldun's Critique of Sufism." *Harvard Middle Eastern and Islamic Review* 8: 242–91.

Mufti, Malik. 2009. "Jihad as Statecraft: Ibn Khaldun on the Conduct of War and Empire." *History of Political Thought* 30(3): 385–410.

———. 2019. "Is Ibn Khaldūn 'Obsessed' with the Supernatural?" *Journal of the American Oriental Society* 139(3): 681–85.

Nakamura, K. 1989. "Ibn Khaldūn's Image of the City." In *Urbanism in Islam, The Proceedings of the International Conference on Urbanism in Islam (ICUIT)*, 301–17. The Middle Eastern Culture Center, Tokyo, Japan, 22–28 October 1989. Tokyo: The Middle Eastern Culture Center.

Nassar, Nassif. 1964. "Le maitre d'Ibn Khaldūn: al-Abili." *Studia Islamica* 20: 103–15.

———. 1967. *La pensée réaliste d'Ibn Khaldūn*. Paris: Presses Universitaires de France.

O'Connor, Timothy, and Christopher Franklin. 2019. "Free Will." In *The Stanford Encyclopedia of Philosophy* (Summer edition), ed. Edward N. Zalta. Retrieved 7 March 2025 from https://plato.stanford.edu/entries/freewill/.

Opwis, Felicitas. 2010. *Maṣlaḥa and the Purpose of the Law: Islamic Discourse on Legal Change from the 4th/10th to 8th/14th Century*. Leiden: Brill.

Özer, Yumna. 2017. "Introduction." In *Ibn Khaldūn on Sufism*. I–xli. Cambridge: The Islamic Texts Society.

Petry, Carl F. 2022. *The Mamluk Sultanate*. Cambridge: Cambridge University Press.

Philipp, Thomas. 2016. "From Rule of Law to Constitutionalism: The Ottoman Context of Arab Political Thought." In *Arabic Thought beyond the Liberal Age*, ed. Jens Hanssen and Max Weiss, 142–65. Cambridge: Cambridge University Press.

Piddington, Ralph. 1957. "Malinowski's Theory of Needs." In *Man and Culture: An Evaluation of the Work of Bronislaw Malinowski*, ed. Raymond Firth, 33–52. London: Routledge & Kegan Paul.

Pines, Shlomo. 1970. "Ibn Khaldūn and Maimonides, a Comparison between Two Texts." *Studia Islamica* 32: 265–74.

Pines, Solomon. 1971. "The Societies Providing for the Bare Necessities of Life according to Ibn Khaldun and the Philosophers." *Studia Islamica* 34: 125–38.

Pišev, Marko. 2019. "Anthropological Aspects of Ibn Khaldun's *Muqaddimah*: A Critical Examination." *Bérose—Encyclopédie internationale des histoires de l'anthropologie*. https://www.berose.fr/article1777.html?lang=fr.

Plutarch. 1919. *The Parallel Lives*, 'The Life of Alexander,' 1.2. Cambridge, MA: Harvard University Press, Loeb Library.

Pomian, Krzysztof. 2006. *Ibn Khaldûn au prisme de l'Occident*. Paris: Gallimard.

Prudovsky, Gad. 1997. "Can We Ascribe to Past Thinkers Concepts They Had No Linguistic Means to Express?" *History and Theory* 36(1): 15–31.

Rabi', Muhammad Mahmoud. 1967. *The Political Theory of Ibn Khaldun*. Leiden: Brill.
Reagan, Ronald. 1993. "There They Go Again." *New York Times*, 18 February: Section A, 23.
Reynolds, Dwight F., ed. 2001. *Interpreting the Self: Autobiography in the Arabic Literary Tradition*. Berkeley: University of California Press.
Robinson, Francis. 2006. "Hero of Islam?" *Times Literary Supplement*, 17 February. Issue 5386: 11.
Rosen, Lawrence. 1971. "Language, History, and the Logic of Inquiry in the Work of LéviStrauss and Sartre." *History and Theory* 10(3): 269–94.
———. 1984. *Bargaining for Reality: The Construction of Social Relations in a Muslim Community*. Chicago: University of Chicago Press.
———. 1989. *The Anthropology of Justice: Law as Culture in Islamic Society*. New York: Cambridge University Press.
———. 2000. *The Justice of Islam*. Oxford: Oxford University Press.
———. 2008. "Theorizing from Within: Ibn Khaldun and the Understanding of Arab Political Culture." In his *Varieties of Muslim Experience*, 121–30. Chicago: University of Chicago Press.
———. 2018a. *Islam and the Rule of Justice*. Chicago: University of Chicago Press.
———. 2018b. *The Judgment of Culture*. London: Routledge.
———. 2024a. "Ibn Khaldūn et l'individu dans l'histoire." In *Ibn Khaldūn et les sciences humaines*, ed. Houari Touati, 305–20. Paris: Editions du Cerf.
———. 2024b. "'My Culture Made Me Do It': Expert Testimony and the Anthropologist's Dilemma." *Current Anthropology* 65(1): 150–66.
Rosenthal, Erwin I. J. 1965. *Islam in the Modern National State*. Cambridge: Cambridge University Press.
Rosenthal, Franz. 1968. "Historiography: Islamic Historiography." In *Encyclopedia of the Social Sciences*, vol. 6, ed. David L. Sills, 407–13. New York: The Macmillan Company and Free Press.
———. 1984. "Ibn Khaldun in His Time." In Bruce Lawrence, ed., *Ibn Khaldun and Islamic Ideology*, 14–26. Leiden: E. J. Brill.
———. 2000. "Ibn Khaldun's Biography Revisited." In *Studies in Honour of Clifford Edmund Bosworth*, vol. 1, ed. Ian Richard Netton, 40–63. Leiden: Brill.
———. 2015. *Man versus Society in Medieval Islam*. Leiden: Brill.
Rouighi, Ramzi. 2019. *Inventing the Berbers: History and Ideology in the Maghrib*. Philadelphia: University of Pennsylvania Press.
Różycki, Tomasz. 2024. *To The Letter*. Brooklyn, NY: Archipelago.
Ruthven, Malise. 2019. "The Otherworldliness of Ibn Khaldun." *New York Review of Books*, 7 February.

Ryder, Norman. 1965. "The Cohort as a Concept in the Study of Social Change." *American Sociological Review* 30: 843–61.

Şahin, Elena. 2024. *The Grand Critic of Ibn Khaldūn: Ibn al-Azraq and His Ideal Sultanate*. Leiden: Brill.

Sahlins, Marshall. 1968. *Tribesmen*. Englewood Cliffs, NJ: Prentice-Hall.

———. 2004. *Apologies to Thucydides: Understanding History as Culture and Vice Versa*. Chicago: University of Chicago Press.

———. 2023. *The New Science of the Enchanted Universe*. Princeton, NJ: Princeton University Press.

Salzman, Philip Carl. 2008. *Culture and Conflict in the Middle East*. Amherst, NY: Humanity Books.

Sapir, Edward. 1985. *Selected Writings in Language, Culture, and Personality*. Berkeley: University of California Press.

Sapolsky, Robert M. 2023. *Determined: A Science of Life Without Free Will*. New York: Penguin.

Shabana, Ayman. 2010. *Custom in Islamic Law and Legal Theory: The Development of the Concepts of 'Urf and 'Adah in the Islamic Legal Tradition*. New York: Palgrave Macmillan.

Shatzmiller, Maya. 1982. *L'historiographie mérinide: Ibn Khaldun et ses contemporaines*. Leiden: Brill.

———. 2000. *The Berbers and the Islamic State: The Marinid Experience in Pre-Protectorate Morocco*. Princeton, NJ: Princeton University Press.

Shehadi, Fadlou. 1984. "Theism, Mysticism and Scientific History in Ibn Khaldun." In *Islamic Philosophy*, ed. Michael E. Marmura, 265–79. Albany: State University of New York Press.

Shterenshis, Michael. 2002. *Tamerlane and the Jews*. London: Routledge.

Singer, Rachel. 2020. "The Black Death in the Maghreb: A Call to Action," *Journal of Medieval Worlds* 2 (3–4): 115–23.

Skalník, Petr, ed. 2022. *Ernest Gellner's Legacy and Social Theory Today*. New York: Palgrave MacMillan.

Smirov, Andrey V. 2021. "Translation as the Manufacturing of Meaning: A Few Words about the Title of Ibn Khaldūn's *History*." *Russian Studies in Philosophy* 58(6): 491–521.

Spengler, Joseph. 1964. "Economic Thought of Islam: Ibn Khaldūn." *Comparative Studies in Society and History* 6: 268–306.

Syrier, Maya. 1947. "Ibn Khaldun and Mysticism." *Islamic Culture* 21(3): 264–302.

Talbi, Mohammed. 1967. "Ibn Haldūn et le sens de l'histoire." *Studia Islamica* 26: 73–148.

———. 1971. "Ibn Khaldun." *Encyclopedia of Islam*, New Edition. 3: 825–31.

———. 1973. *Ibn Khaldūn et l'histoire*. Tunis: Maison Tunisienne de l' Édition.
Time Magazine. 1947. "Letter from the Publisher." 28 April. Retrieved 7 March 2025 from https://content.time.com/time/subscriber/article/0,33009,793546-1,00.html.
Tomar, Cengiz. 2008. "Between Myth and Reality: Approaches to Ibn Khaldun in the Arab World." *Asian Journal of Social Science* 36(3–4): 590–611.
Touati, Houari, ed. 2024. *Ibn Khaldūn et les sciences humaines: La mediation du naturalism*. Paris: Editions Cerf.
Toynbee, Arnold J. 1934. *A Study of History*, vol. 3. Oxford: Oxford University Press.
———. 1954. *A Study of History*, vol. 10. Oxford: Oxford University Press.
Trabelsi, Bouraoui. 2003. "Les jardins d'agrément dans la *Muqaddima* d'Ibn Khaldûn." *IBLA* [Tunis], vol. 66 année, 1/2003, no. 191: 35–51.
Tse, Peter Ulric. 2013. *The Neural Basis of Free Will: Criterial Causation*. Cambridge, MA: The MIT Press.
Turner, Bryan. 1971. "Sociological Founders and Precursors: The Theories of Religion of Émile Durkheim, Fustel de Coulanges and Ibn Khaldūn." *Religion* 1: 32–48.
United Nations Development Programme. 2005. *Arab Human Development Report 2004*. New York: United Nations.
Valensi, Lucette. 2010. "La découverte d'un grand auteur en Europe." In *Figures d'Ibn Khaldûn: Reception, appropriation et usages*, ed. Houari Touati, 111–36. Algiers: CNRPAH.
Van Steenbergen, Jo. 2022. "Rethinking 'the Mamlūk State' with Ibn Khaldūn: 'Mamlukization,' *'aṣabiyya*, and Historiographical Imaginations of the Sultanate of Cairo (1200s–1500s)." In *The Historian of Islam at Work*, ed. Letizia Ostia and Maaike van Berkel, 117–39. Leiden: Brill.
Verza, Annalisa. 2019. "The Senility of Group Solidarity and Contemporary Multiculturalism: A Word of Warning from a Medieval Arabic Thinker." *Ratio Juris* 32(1) 76–101.
———. 2021. *Ibn Khaldun and the Arab Origins of the Sociology of Civilisation and Power*. Cham, Switzerland: Springer.
Von Sivers, P. 1980. "Back to Nature: The Agrarian Foundations of Society according to Ibn Khaldûn." *Arabica* 28(1): 68–91.
Waller, Bruce N. 2011. *Against Moral Responsibility*. Cambridge, MA: The MIT Press.
White, Hayden V. 1959. "Ibn Khaldun in World Philosophy of History." *Comparative Studies in Society and History* 2(1): 110–25.

White, Leslie. 1959. *The Evolution of Culture*. New York: McGraw-Hill Book Co.

Whitehouse, Harvey. 2024. *Inheritance: The Evolutionary Origins of the Modern World*. New York: Hutchinson Heinemann.

Willis, John R. 2004. "Beasts, Jinn and Angels: The 'Virtual' World of Ibn Khaldun." *The Maghreb Review* 29(1–4): 53–61.

Wolfson, Harry A. 1959. "Ibn Khaldun on Attributes and Predestination." *Speculum* 34(4): 585–97.

Zuckerberg, Mark. 2015. "A Year of Books." *Facebook*, 1 June. Retrieved 7 March 2025 from https://www.facebook.com/pages/Muqaddimah/107640942598547/.

BROADCAST INTERVIEWS AND ONLINE VIDEOS

Ibn Khaldun. 2010. BBC Program hosted by Melvyn Bragg, with guests Robert G. Hoyland, Robert Irwin, and Hugh N. Kennedy. 4 February. Retrieved 7 March 2025 from https://www.bbc.co.uk/programmes/b00qckbw.

Ibn Khaldun: 14th Century Sage. 2019. BBC Program "The Forum," with Syed Farid al-Attas, Josephine van den Bent, and Robert Irwin. 12 December. Retrieved 7 March 2025 from https://www.bbc.co.uk/sounds/play/w3csyp5t.

Ibn Khaldun's 'The Muqaddimah': The Best Book You've Never Read. 2021. CUNY Graduate Center, Interview with Aziz al-Azmeh. 20 December. Retrieved 7 March 2025 from https://www.gc.cuny.edu/news/ibn-khalduns-muqaddimah-best-book-youve-never-read-aziz-al-azmeh.

Ibn Khaldun and Dune: Desert Culture, Asabiyya and Religion. 2021. Retrieved 7 March 2025 from https://www.reddit.com/r/dune/comments/r4inup/herbert_was_greatly_inspired_by_the_14th_century/.

Ibn Khaldun and Early Muslim Strategic Thought. 2022. A Conversation with Malik Mufti conducted by Beatrice Heuser and Paul O'Neill. The Royal United Services Institute for Defence and Security Studies | RUSI. 8 November. Retrieved 7 March 2025 from https://www.rusi.org/podcasts/talking-strategy/episode-4-ibn-khaldun-and-early-muslim-strategic-thought.

New Wave History. 2024. "Asabiyya: The Significance of the Tribe in Islamic Culture. Interview with Dr. Akbar Ahmed." *YouTube*, uploaded 15 August. https://www.youtube.com/watch?v=lxDiomuew9E.

INDEX

Abu Yahya (Ibn Khaldun's brother), 23
Ahmed, Akbar, 52–3, 131
Almohad dynasty, 16, 50, 55
Almoravid dynasty, 16, 50
anthropology, 1–2, 8, 30, 74–7
Arabic language, 40
'asabiya (group solidarity), 40–56, 78n4, 84–5, 113, 128, 132
    translations, 41
    leadership, 44, 68, 128–9

Bedouin, *See* nomads
Berber dynasties, 16–21, 50, 53
biography and autobiography, 4
Black Death, 9, 16–18, 51

cohorts, 50–1

Durkheim, Emile, 53–4

free will, 61–82
    philosophical and anthropological literature, 74–77
    See also Ibn Khaldun, free will

Gellner, Ernest, 52

Hafsid dynasty, 19, 21, 23

Ibn Khaldun
    anthropologist, 1, 30, 65
    Aristotle, 31, 38, 45, 47, 84, 134
    commemorations of his birth, 7–8
    concept of time, 123–25
    corruption in courts, 100–3, 118n6
    criticism of other historians, 37–8
    cyclical view of history, 2, 9, 36–56, 68, 123, 134
    dualities, 84
    evolution and Great Chain of Being, 125
    free will, 61–82
    genealogy, 14, 42–3, 46, 58n15
    hierarchy of knowledge, 70
    history, accidents of, 45–6
    human nature, 37–39, 42, 44, 62–4, 70–1, 84–5, 125–6
    influence on anthropologists, 51–6, 95, 116–17, 129, 131
    institutions, 68
    judge, 10, 25, 28, 99–100, 106, 114
    mysticism, 86–9, 92, 109–10
    negotiator, 20, 22, 31
    non-Muslims, 89–90
    personal character, 19, 22, 24, 32–3
    psychological views, 125–8
    religion, 84–98
    style of explanation, 2, 5–6, 104–5, 134
    uncertainty, 72–3
inheritance law, 111–13
Islam
    chaos (*fitna*), 69
    end of, 120n20

free will, 61-2
 pilgrimage, 62
 Mahdi, 64, 79n8, 85
Islamic law, 24, 67-8, 72, 99-121
 customary law, 106-9
 inheritance, 112-13
 justice, 43, 113-14
 religious endowments, 111-12

kingship, 55, 67

Lisan ad-Din al-Khatib, 20-22, 29

Mahdi, *See* Ibn Khaldun, Mahdi
Mamluks, 25, 50, 99-100
Merinid dynasty, 16, 18, 21
Muqaddima, 3-4
 writing of, 22-24, 65

nomads, 39-40, 47, 55, 59n17, 63, 109

Ottomans, 60n21

persons, concept of, 115, 126-7
philosophers, 73-5
prophets and prophecy, 68

ritual inversion, 65

speculation (*naẓar*), 2, 105
Sufism, 28, 71, 85-6, 92-4, 110
 See also Ibn Khaldun, religion

Tamerlane (Timur), 13, 25-28, 32, 50, 64, 66, 88
taxation, 48-49, 51
teachers, 45, 69, 71-2
Toynbee, Arnold, 6
tribes, 43, 47, 54

universals and particulars, 106, 130

www.ingramcontent.com/pod-product-compliance
Lightning Source LLC
Chambersburg PA
CBHW071710020426
42333CB00017B/2204